Applications of the Myers-Briggs Type Indicator in Counseling:

A Casebook

JUDITH A. PROVOST, ED.D.

CENTER FOR APPLICATIONS OF
PSYCHOLOGICAL TYPE INC.

Published by Center for Applications of Psychological Type Inc.

Copyright © 1993 by Judith A. Provost

Second Edition 1993

[MBTI is a registered Trade Mark,
Consulting Psychologists Press Inc., Palo Alto, CA]

Library of Congress Cataloging-in-Publications Data

Provost, Judith A., 1942-
A casebook: applications of the Myers-Briggs Type Indicatior in counseling/Judith A. Provost.—2nd ed.

p. cm.

Includes bibliographical refereces.

ISBN 0-935652-17-5
    1. Myers-Briggs Type Indicator.   2. Counseling.   I. Title,
BF698.8.M94P76 1993
155.2'64—dc20   93-41360
                                                                      CIP

"For my family, who
taught me the
most about Type."

Contents

Preface

This edition is a major rewriting of the original book. In the ten years since I first wrote about counseling with the Myers-Brigg Type Indicator, some of the thinking about type theory and the way we talk about type have changed. Ten more years of clinical experience have added to my understanding of using the MBTI. Every chapter was expanded to reflect this experience and these changes. The chapter about type development doubled in size to add more depth about the inferior function, mid-life issues, and implications of type development for counseling. The chapter on using the MBTI in counseling also doubled to include information on type dynamics within the counseling process. The most important addition in this chapter is a section on multicultural counseling as it relates to type. The eighteen cases have been rewritten to improve clarity and clean up out-of-date language. I've added a lengthy chapter on couples counseling, with couples defined broadly as committed relationships whether gay or straight, married or living together. New research findings related to counseling have been added to the last chapter.

The original casebook came to be written after several years of writing cases in my head as I drove to work or made the long drive to Gainesville during doctoral studies. It was Mary McCaulley who encouraged me to get the cases down on paper. Besides Mary, I have type theory to thank for helping me to get organized, arrange an appropriate work rhythm for my ENFP style, and find motivators to help me complete the project once I started. One of the most useful aspects of the MBTI is its dynamic theory which allows for, and encourages, growth and change within basic personality types.

When this casebook was first conceived, there was some question as to whether cases should come from the practices of a variety of practitioners or from a single practitioner. I decided to present cases only from my own practice to give the casebook continuity and flow and to demonstrate how one therapist, with a given MBTI type and counseling orientation, worked with all 16 types. This is both a strength and a limitation of the book. There is probably an ENFP bias in my counseling approach and descriptions because of my own particular "lense." My vocabulary, metaphors, and examples are obviously influenced by my type.

A brief description of my clinical orientation and experience with the Myers-Briggs Type Indicator may be helpful to readers in weighing the usefulness of this casebook. My professional degrees include a master's degree in community mental health nursing from UCLA and the Ed.D. from the University of Florida's Department of Counselor Education. I have worked in psychiatric hospitals, community mental health centers, and college settings. I have had a private practice in career counseling and psychotherapy and have done some consulting with organizations, utilizing the MBTI. My counseling orientation is primarily existential with a Gestalt approach. I borrow from other approaches, such as cognitive, behavioral, and family systems as needed to help a specific client.

I discovered the MBTI in my first college counseling position in 1974 and quickly became enthusiastic about its possibilities and hungry for more knowledge about the instrument. About that time CAPT (Center for Applications of Psychological Type) under Mary McCaulley's leadership and with Isabel Briggs Myers' support, was solidifying the professional use of the MBTI. In 1975, I attended the first international conference on the MBTI held in Gainesville, Florida. This conference and subsequent MBTI conferences and workshops have stimulated me to utilize the MBTI in my private and college practices and in conducting research. I have led MBTI workshops on national, regional, and local levels.

As Director of Counseling Services, and for five years also Director of Health Services, at a four year liberal arts college, I have systematically administered the MBTI to all entering freshmen during orientation week. Because most students remain at the college for four years and live on campus, I have been able to "type watch," observing first-hand the dynamic development of young types over this four year period. Type development is at the core of MBTI theory and certainly at the core of counseling applications. These observations of young adults have given me an understanding of what is necessary for good type development, as well as what will impede that development. In this living laboratory, which is a residential college, the effects of counseling interventions, of environmental factors, and of life events on the various types can be observed. Socialization and relationship patterns of the 16 types can also be followed. The stages and tasks identified in developmental psychology and the theory of type development together form an extremely useful framework for counseling and therapy.

I am grateful to all the young people and clients who have enriched my life by allowing me to know them and to share in their discoveries. With this book I share these discoveries with you, the reader, and hope you will find some useful ideas for your own practice. I treasure the many stimulating MBTI discussions with professional associates, especially with my APT and CAPT friends. A special thanks to Mary McCaulley, who enriches us all in our quest for fuller understanding of type.

Judith A. Provost, Ed.D.
New Smyrna Beach, Florida

CHAPTER ONE

Introduction

This casebook is written for counselors and therapists who have already had an introduction to the Myers-Briggs Type Indicator. Readers should know their own type and have a basic knowledge of the four preference scales and Carl Jung's theory of psychological types. They should also be familiar with the psychometric properties, administration, and interpretation of the instrument.

This casebook is not a substitute for reading the MBTI *Manual* or taking a workshop on the theory and use of the MBTI. Excellent materials exist for important background reading. I particularly recommend Isabel Briggs Myers' *Gifts Differing* (1980) for a sound and thorough, yet very readable, presentation of type. Furthermore, it is assumed that readers who are practitioners will already have training in the use of psychometric instruments and a model for conducting counseling and therapy. It is assumed that practitioners already have some knowledge of therapies such as Gestalt and Rational Emotive Therapy; therefore these therapies will not be elaborated on when cited as approaches to certain of the cases.

This casebook will demonstrate applications of the MBTI in counseling/psychotherapy with individuals and with couples. Chapter Four contains eighteen cases of individual counseling, representing various types, ages and presenting problems. Chapter Five shows ways of using the Indicator with couples. Through these applications, readers can gain a deeper understanding of type dynamics and type development and perhaps some new ideas for using type in their own practices. Selection of the specific cases for the book was made from my years of private and college counseling practice. Of the many possible cases, those were chosen which best exemplified the typical kinds of problems I encounter working with each of the 16 types. There are more college-age clients (18-24) represented here, because these cases vividly demonstrate type development problems and the relationship of type to counseling interventions.

Because of these selection factors, these clients are above average intelligence and are, for the most part, in earlier stages of type development than an older population. For example, a young ISTJ may demonstrate somewhat different characteristics than an older ISTJ because there has been less time to develop all the functions. Young ISTJs may appear more narrow in interests and coping style. They may view the world in "black and white" arbitrary terms and may expect definitive answers from authority figures.

Mature ISTJs are likely to respect authority and tradition, yet be independent-minded. Mature ISTJs are open to possibilities and more flexible in their approach to life.

Chapter Two, "Type Development and Counseling," shows how age and environment (including multicultural factors) affect the development and expression of type. This chapter is an important foundation on which the rest of the book is based. Included in this discussion are the importance of understanding the nature of dominant, auxiliary, and inferior functions; counseling problems related to type development; and special considerations surrounding the inferior function and mid-life.

Chapter Three, "Using the MBTI in Counseling," explores the MBTI in relation to counseling settings, counseling goals, administration and interpretation, ethics of use, the counseling process, and multicultural issues. The latter two topics are new to this edition and are particularly relevant to the work of counselor/therapists today.

The last chapter, Six, "Type Patterns in Counseling: Research and Conclusions," includes some of the new studies on frequencies of types in various kinds of counseling. Caution should be used when interpreting these data, since most MBTI studies related to counseling use samples of convenience and a wide array of methodologies. It becomes difficult to compare findings from various studies or to generalize findings to larger populations. We also must resist using the MBTI as a diagnostic tool for emotional problems and psychopathology. Myers' purpose and approach in developing the MBTI was to address normal development. This chapter may suggest some general *tendencies* of certain types, but the important message of this book is how type can be facilitative to the client and to the counseling process.

CHAPTER TWO

Type Development and Counseling

The Dominant and Auxiliary

By understanding psychological type development and the individuation process, counselors have a great deal of information
beyond merely identifying four MBTI preferences to help them
in assessing and intervening with clients. Type theory postulates that
everyone has four basic mental functions or processes: two perception
functions (Sensing, S, and Intuition, N) and two judgment functions
(Thinking, T, and Feeling, F). Individuals differ in the priority or preference they give each function and in the order in which they develop
these functions. In other words, for different types there is a different
developmental order and degree of use of these four functions.

The most preferred or favorite function is called the dominant. The
second favorite is the auxiliary and serves as a complementary and balancing function to the dominant. Balance, however, does not mean giving equal energy to both functions. The dominant usually claims the
majority of an individual's energy, while the auxiliary will complement
it in two ways. If the dominant is a perception function (S or N), the
auxiliary will be a judging function (T or F), or vice versa. The second
kind of balance is through expression of the auxiliary in the opposite
attitude (Extraversion, E, or Introversion, I) from the dominant. If the
dominant is extraverted, the auxiliary is introverted or vice versa.
Through this balance the individual has a mental function for perceiving and one for judging, with one of these used for dealing with the
extraverted (outer) world and one for dealing with the introverted
(inner) world. In several of the clinical cases described in Chapter
Four, the lack of a developed auxiliary was associated with client imbal-
ance and difficulty. For example, a client with dominant N and without

3

a balancing T or F auxiliary might plunge into a great number of projects without being able to evaluate whether the projects are appropriate or not.

Extraversion-Introversion (E-I) and Judgment-Perception (J-P) are attitudes, as opposed to functions. These attitudes point to an individual's dominant and auxiliary and indicate how these functions are used. The J-P scale, Myers' contribution to Jung's theory of psychological types, reflects the preferred functional style for dealing with the outer world. People with a judgment preference use a judgment function (T or F) to evaluate and order their outer lives. People preferring perception use a perception function (S or N) to discover and experience their outer life spontaneously. The J-P dimension identifies the dominant function for extraverts because by definition extraverts use their dominant function in the extraverted/outer world. For introverts, the J-P dimension points to the auxiliary, since by definition introverts use their dominant function in the inner/introverted world. Using ENFJ and INFJ for examples, the J in both types points to the judging function, feeling. For the ENFJ, feeling is the dominant because it is the function used in the outer world. For the INFJ, feeling is the auxiliary, because for introverts the second favorite function is used in the outer world while the dominant, here intuition, is used in the inner world.

THE TERTIARY AND INFERIOR

Now that the dominant and auxiliary are identified, the tertiary and inferior can also be identified. The tertiary is the polar opposite function to the auxiliary. For ENFJ, the opposite to intuition auxiliary is sensing, the tertiary. For INFJ, the opposite of auxiliary feeling is thinking, the tertiary. The inferior function is the polar opposite of the dominant. For ENFJ, the opposite to dominant feeling is thinking inferior. For INFJ, the opposite to dominant intuition is sensing inferior.

Thus, the four scales have a combined effect; "the whole is greater than the sum of its parts." Each of the 16 types is a specific developmental map indicating the natural order of function development, the preferred and least preferred functions, and how they are used in the inner and outer worlds. To reinforce this explanation, each case in Chapter Four will have a notation to indicate the order of function development. For example, the notation for an ESTJ will look like this:

EXTRAVERTED THINKING
with Sensing

ESTJ

T

S

N

F

"Extraverted Thinking" means that thinking is the dominant function and is extraverted, or used in dealing with the outer world. " With sensing," means sensing is the auxiliary function and is introverted. The functions are listed in descending order from dominant #1, T, to inferior #4, F. "Introverted thinking with sensing" (ISTP), means that the dominant function, thinking, is introverted and the auxiliary, sensing, is extraverted.

Type Development Over the Lifespan

Usually individuals develop their dominant function first and begin this development in childhood. Von Franz (1979), explaining Jung's theory, states that the dominant should be reflected in behavior by kindergarten age. Individuals direct most of their energy and attention to activities and interests which strengthen their favored function. Because this function comes naturally, individuals meet with success and obtain reinforcement for use of this function. Thus, they become specialists in that function. For example, in childhood those with dominant N might prefer games of imagination and make-believe, receive much adult attention for their incredible stories, perhaps develop creative writing ability, get rewarded by teachers for creative work, and so on. These individuals with dominant N might pay little attention to S activities and interests such as mechanical or intricately detailed hobbies.

As individuals develop their dominant function, they also typically begin exercising their auxiliary. Auxiliary development usually begins in adolescence, but there is no specific time-table other than the sequence itself. Introverts may develop their auxiliary function at the same time they are developing their dominant because of a need to have a function for dealing with the outer world. Extraverts do not have this same necessity since their dominant is used in the outer world. Thus one is more likely to find introverted adolescents with both auxiliary and dominant developed than to find this among extraverted types.

Environmental and Multicultural Factors

Readiness and environmental factors influence the timing of these developments. If the environment is nonsupportive or inhibiting of the expression of a certain function or type, that function may develop more slowly and not according to the sequence just described. An INFP boy, for example, from a very traditional home where males were expected to have "macho" interests such as football and military activities might be put down or discouraged from interests such as creative writing and art. He might be inhibited from exploring and developing his dominant feeling function and have to rely on intuition auxiliary and even sensing. The result of postponing development of the dominant may be a lack of confidence, direction, or a clear sense of self. Abusive, controlling, or dysfunctional homes can inhibit type development. Sometimes merely being a minority type (the only one) in the family can inhibit development unless the family is accepting and respectful of the difference.

Cultural, racial, and gender factors can shape how type develops and how it is reported on the MBTI. Individuals within a minority culture may not feel safe to express their true MBTI preferences and for survival may have to use less preferred functions. For example, a young African-American man with preferences for ESFP comes out ISTJ when taking the MBTI in a predominantly white environment. There are two issues here: one, what is his true type? and two, has the environment allowed him to gain confidence in expressing and using his actual preferences? He may be undeveloped because of a nonsupportive environment.

Stress in the environment may affect the way individuals, such as this African-American, answer the MBTI. A recent study by Ware and Rytting (1993) found that a sample of college students reported a shift towards preferences for I, S, and T under conditions of stress.

Of course, one cannot assume that people of color or of any background different from the predominant culture have been inhibited in their development. Counselors would need to look carefully at issues of diversity and *context* with each client individually. A specific culture can discourage certain preferences. Just as the male INFP within a traditional "macho" culture was discouraged from developing his dominant feeling, an ENTP young woman from a traditional Hispanic background was discouraged from developing her dominant extraverted intuition. Her culture disapproved of her enterprising, outspoken, breaking from tradition tendencies ; these were not acceptable behaviors for women in her family. Because of these environmental inhibitors, this woman did not develop confidence in her dominant and auxiliary until her late twenties. Diversity issues and type are discussed further in relation to counseling in Chapter Three.

The Inferior and Development

The natural pattern of development, then, is from dominant to auxiliary to tertiary (the function opposite the auxiliary) and to the inferior or least preferred (opposite the dominant). The latter is sometimes referred to as the "shadow," because it is so difficult to access and is so primitive. It is probably more accurate to say that the third and fourth functions exist primarily in the shadow, because these functions are primitive and not under the same conscious control as the dominant and auxiliary. Shadow was a term used by Jung to describe aspects of oneself that are unconscious and unrecognized. The term "least preferred function" has a less negative connotation for the client than the term "inferior." If and when #4 (and #3) can be utilized in mature adulthood, the outcome is often positive, even exhilarating.

Von Franz, Jung and others have speculated that most people may not truly begin to develop the fourth function until later in life, and at best it will always remain an elusive aspect of the personality. The path to transcending oneself, to obtaining heightened awareness and even a new sense of spirituality, is found when accessing the less preferred functions. Most successful meditation approaches create ways to access the fourth function.

The tertiary and inferior functions can be a source of spiritual renewal or of personal satisfaction under positive developmental conditions but can also be a source of great distress under highly stressful conditions. When individuals are physically ill, exhausted, and stressed beyond normal levels, their least preferred function or functions are likely to emerge and "swamp" the normal operation of dominant and auxiliary functions. It's as if the conscious functions of the psyche become exhausted or overloaded and the primitive functions take over, but without a sense of control. In these situations individuals report feeling "beside myself" or feel a "split" as if they were "a Dr. Jekyll and Mr. Hyde." Clients who present in crisis may be "in the grip of the inferior function." Counselors can be misled by these first impressions of clients, since they are not seeing the usual ego functioning personality. Some examples of signs of the inferior grip are:

When sensing is dominant and intuition is inferior—catastrophic imaginings, taking one small fact and blowing it way out of proportion, projecting and generalizing negative possibilities into the future.

When intuition is dominant and sensing is inferior—becoming obsessive-compulsive about details, becoming hypochondriacal by focusing on a specific body sensation, becoming extremely nit-picking and hypersensitive to the environment.

When thinking is dominant and feeling is inferior—becoming overly sentimental, generalizing that no one cares and the individual doesn't "belong," expressing feeling "wounded" or "attacked."

When feeling is dominant and thinking is inferior—becoming extremely critical either of self or others, lashing out in a harsh cutting manner, withdrawing from people with a show of irritation.

In my experience the best way to help clients in the grip of their inferior is to engage their auxiliary function. It is essential to get clients back into their conscious functions where they have control. It seems too big a shift to go from the inferior straight to the opposite pole, the dominant, so the auxiliary is a likely intermediate step. An example is the case of Tom, ENFJ, in Chapter Four. Tom directed harsh criticism at himself, which immobilized him (inferior thinking). His intuition auxiliary was engaged to look at patterns in his relationships and in the conditions which set off this harsh internal critic. From the auxiliary he was able to also get back to his dominant feeling so he could function from his strengths.

Some of these examples show the importance to counselors of understanding type dynamics and the nature of dominant and inferior functions. Because of these dynamics it is usually unwise to use a counseling intervention that engages the inferior function early in the counseling relationship or when clients are under stress. Engaging the inferior instead of the dominant and auxiliary can lead to increased anxiety and can further destabilize clients. For example, in working with clients who were dominant sensing, it would not usually be therapeutic to do guided imagery or active imagination in the early stages of counseling or when these clients were highly anxious. Inferior intuition might become activated and create additional difficulty for these clients.

Type Development and Presenting Problems

From our discussion of the lifelong type development process, it becomes clear that expression of type will vary somewhat depending on client age and environmental background. When working with young clients (adolescents and young adults), we can't assume development of both dominant and auxiliary. Many young clients have difficulties requiring counseling in part because they have not yet developed both dominant and auxiliary functions. One counseling intervention, therefore, is to encourage development of both of these functions.

Another type difficulty in clients can be the complete avoidance of the least preferred (tertiary and inferior) functions. This avoidance can lead to career and other life difficulties and low self-esteem. Avoidance of the least preferred functions can lead to overuse and inappropriate employment of the favored functions. These clients may lack a "well-rounded" presence and seem to take an unbalanced approach to life. Counselors can assist these clients to become aware of the dynamics of this avoidance and the consequences. Together they can explore ways of beginning to become more comfortable with the tertiary and inferior functions. Although young clients cannot be expected to have much conscious use of third and fourth functions, they can be encouraged to learn small, careful ways to activate these functions instead of completely avoiding them.

An example of persistent avoidance of the inferior function and resultant difficulties is the case of Brenda, a college student. Brenda confirmed her type preferences for INTP. One of her concerns which brought her to counseling was her discomfort and subsequent avoidance of relationships with her peers. She was reasonably comfortable relating to her professors (primarily INTJs) in the defined role of serious student but did not know how to "hang out" with peers in the residence hall. She had difficulty reading others' reactions, interpreting communications, and knowing how to respond appropriately. These interpersonal skills required some use of her inferior feeling function. Because she didn't feel interpersonally competent, and competence is a crucial condition for NTs, she avoided interactions with peers. The result was social isolation and a sense of alienation. The counselor approached this problem through cause-and-effect analysis to engage Brenda's dominant thinking function. Together they explored ways of "making friends" with her inferior feeling function. Interpersonal skills were shaped in counseling sessions through role-playing and modeling. Homework to practice these skills outside counseling was assigned.

With clients who are middle-aged or older the type issues are usually different. Jung said every issue at mid-life and thereafter is a spiritual one. By this he did not refer to religion in the traditional sense. He was referring to the crucial individuation work of the latter half of life as individuals strive towards wholeness and a fuller sense of themselves. This striving has a spiritual quality and urgency, often difficult for clients to articulate but pressing enough to bring them into counseling. Often these clients will self-identify as experiencing "mid-life crisis" or some sort of search.

By mid-life most people have developed and learned to use effectively their dominant and auxiliary. Their type related discomfort is likely to occur in one of two ways. They may be "stuck" in their careers and in their lives—repeating themes and patterns in relationships and in their lifestyles. They persist in doing "more of the same" relying exclusively on their dominant and auxiliary and on past coping style. This stuckness may be a reflection of an unrecognized need to grow and develop other parts of themselves, to develop a broader behavioral repertoire, including type dimensions other than their preferences. Or, instead of being "stuck," middle-aged clients may feel extremely "restless" and behave as if in a second adolescence. There is an unconscious drive to claim more parts of themselves and grow beyond their old selves.

In both cases, clients do not usually need encouragement to use their preferred functions, which are closely identified with their persona and conscious self. Rather what they need is help with their least preferred functions. Murray Stein (1985), a Jungian analyst, describes the mid-life period as a time of breaking down the old ego structures of the persona and incorporating into consciousness more of the unconscious or shadow, unclaimed parts of the self. The third and fourth functions are some of these parts. Breaking down the old persona or image in order to incorporate these previously unconscious parts leads to an expanded sense of self, a sense of growth and renewal, often described by individuals as "spiritual."

Some of the tasks involved in breaking down the old and incorporating the new are:

∝ Reconciling our dreams with reality; at mid-life the realities of our actual existence challenge our idealized plans for career, family, and lifestyle.
∝ Realizing our own finiteness and mortality; we have limited time left to accomplish our goals and achieve our dreams.
∝ Working through the deterioration or loss of our parents, an illusionary buffer between us and death.
∝ Accepting changes and the aging process within our own bodies.
∝ Discovering that there is more to life than our early assumptions and values allowed; making new meaning.
∝ Different types approach these tasks differently.

Some clients resist these tasks and "dig in their heels" developmentally. They fear change within themselves and others. I have seen this reaction most frequently with SJ types although I've known other types to respond this way as well. Individuals with the sensing judging combination tend to hold on to their current realities and tradition. Even if they are dissatisfied with aspects of their lives, they prefer the familiar to the unknown, the present structure of their lives to opening up to new possibilities. SJs can be helped to deal with mid-life issues by first acknowledging their needs for structure and order. Their approach to change may be more deliberative and slow, step by step, talking out specific issues with the counselor. Counselors can help these clients see the patterns and themes inherent in these life tasks.

Without help in facing these mid-life changes many individuals become stuck in their growth. In trying to hold on to the old familiar ways, they may become brittle and defended. By brittle I mean the opposite of flexible and open to new learnings. The brittle person struggles to preserve an outdated persona held together by resistance to change, denial, and so on. Brittle individuals are more subject to organic disease as well as emotional problems and relationship difficulties. Myocardial infarcts are the kind of disease that may be associated with stuck, brittle individuals. One study by Roberts and Roberts (1988) found SJ types with a statistically significant higher rate of heart attacks. Although heart disease has many causes, personality and changes at mid-life may contribute to its incidence.

Some types may approach the mid-life crisis with an "everything is up for grabs" attitude. ENTP and ENFP types, for example, who by nature tend to be restless and fascinated by change, may shed their earlier personas and experiment with their lives. Their response can be the opposite extreme to those who dig in and become brittle. In being open to change these individuals may completely discard the life structure that has worked for them in the past. Their lives—careers, relationships, lifestyles—may become chaotic. Others may perceive them as "clearly in their second adolescence." Counselors can assist these clients in understanding the tasks at mid-life and the needs of their types. Together they can explore the value of incorporating more of the inferior sensing and the tertiary judging function into their conscious lives. These clients need assistance in balancing change and flexibility with some kinds of constants or structures to ground them in reality (sensing).

These type dynamics and developmental issues become important when working with clients, since interventions should utilize already existing coping mechanisms and strengths as well as encouraging development of the other MBTI functions. Identifying strengths is particularly helpful in crisis situations. If a therapist is working with an ESTJ client, the therapist must first appeal to the client's sense of logic (T) and secondly give concrete examples (S) in structuring interventions. Clients who appear to rely too heavily or exclusively on one function, usually the dominant, can be helped to develop more balance through exercising one of the other functions as well. One general counseling goal is to help clients develop all their functions so that they are capable of using the function appropriate to a given situation. Of course, there is a maturational factor here which prevents therapists from being able to artificially move clients further along in their development before they are ready. For example, the counselor may identify the need to develop one of the judging functions, but the client may not be ready or willing to work toward that end. The therapist, however, can offer guidance and opportunities to help the individual in developing the other functions. The process may be very gradual and continue long after therapy is terminated.

Another benefit of knowing a client's type is anticipating potential areas of difficulty. From type theory, counselors will have certain hypotheses about client behavior, coping style, and developmental tasks or problems. These hypotheses can be checked out in counseling sessions. For example, the counselor could anticipate that a young INTP might have difficulty relating to peers. Here the dominant function is T and the least preferred, and most likely undeveloped, is F. To his peers he might appear eccentric, reticent, puzzling, strongly individualistic, and possibly antisocial. Note the stress on "might." One cannot determine the actual level of development of the other functions without interview data and ongoing observations. Another INTP may utilize intuition effectively to see the patterns in his relationships and find creative ways to interact with others and still preserve his individuality. The MBTI reflects a dynamic, not static, theory of personality and as an instrument is thus more of a guide than a diagnostic tool.

In summary, this chapter has presented a model for personality development based on type theory. Each of the 16 types is a dynamic map of an individual's development from the dominant function, to the auxiliary, to the third, and finally to the least preferred function. Environmental factors may interfere with this natural order and slow down development.

Developmental issues can be explored with clients through the following questions:

1. Does the client have a developed dominant function and confidence in using this function? If not, the client may be inconsistent and ineffective in dealing with life.

2. Does the client have a developed auxiliary function called into play as appropriate to complement the dominant so that the client can use both perception and judgment and operate in both the extraverted and introverted attitudes?

3. In which functions does the client have confidence? Is the client able to use any other functions other than the preferred ones as situations demand, or does the client consistently avoid certain situations and tasks with problematic consequences?

4. Can the client use all four functions (S, N, T, F) in decision making?

5. If the client has little or no use of certain functions, how willing is the client to work on this?

6. For the client's age is he/she less developed than would be expected based on Jung's theory of individuation? Are there environmental factors such as early childhood trauma and family relationships which may be inhibiting development?

Everyone has the potential for developing and utilizing all four functions over the lifespan. Counselors can assist in this development. Clients' MBTI type should be viewed in the broader context of their age, environment, and stage of personal growth. Type does not stand on its own but must be seen in context because of its interactive, dynamic nature. Chapter Three will expand on appropriate use of the MBTI.

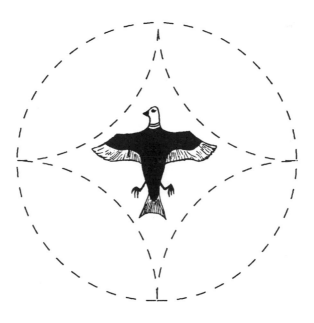

CHAPTER THREE

Using the MBTI in Counseling

Professionals are encouraged to think through their use of the MBTI in terms of appropriate settings, purposes or outcomes desired, timing of administration, appropriate clients, and ethics. The MBTI should not be used indiscriminately or in "cookbook" fashion. Comments here serve as a supplement to, but not a substitute for, training in MBTI administration and interpretation.

SETTINGS

The MBTI is valuable in many settings, in the private practice of counseling and psychotherapy, in community agencies, in consultation with organizations and businesses, and in educational institutions. The instrument can be administered to individuals or groups. In my primary setting, a college, the MBTI is usually group administered, along with several academic placement tests, to all freshmen during orientation week. Students who miss this group administration may take the MBTI by appointment at any time.

Example of Use in a College Setting

Before giving the standardized instructions for taking the Indicator, I introduce myself and the use of the MBTI. Freshmen are told that the results will be available to them within a few weeks to aid in adjustment to college, in choosing academic majors, and in career planning. They are told that when the results are back they will receive a memo with the counseling center phone number so they can make appointments for interpretation at their convenience. Confidentiality is stressed. Results are only available and released to the individual students themselves.

Many freshmen come in for interpretation within a few months of receiving the memo, but many wait until their sophomore year. To enhance the outreach, freshman advisors are also informed that MBTI results are available to their advisees. Thus, in student-advisor conversations about academic direction and adjustment, the advisor can suggest a meeting with one of the counselors to explore these issues in light of MBTI results. It is up to the student to decide whether to share results with the advisor. Many freshmen who seek interpretation have underlying counseling needs, and the MBTI is an excuse for them to make an appointment. In this way, the MBTI is a good counseling outreach and point of contact, however brief. Some students will have one session about their results and return months later to work on personal problems. Trust and mutual respect had been established in that first visit for MBTI results. Following the memo, when requests for appointments are high, the counseling center may group several students together for interpretation. Students do not seem to mind the small group and are invited to come back for further individual consultation if they so desire. I prefer individual interpretive appointments, when time allows, because of the better opportunity for exploration.

If students delay in obtaining their results for a year or two, caution should be used in interpretation because of the time lapse. There may be some change over time in the way students (or any individuals) report their type. Although individuals' "true" types theoretically do not change, such factors as increased self-awareness, transition stresses, and the break from parents can influence the way individuals report their preferences. Therefore, descriptions of the preferences are checked out carefully against clients' self-perceptions and counselor observations. Students are offered the opportunity to retake the MBTI, especially if there is any doubt, or if preferences are unclear. The *Manual* includes a lengthy chapter on the many reliability studies done for both test-retest and internal consistency. Reliability is good to excellent for adolescents and adults with average or better intelligence and reading levels of eighth grade or higher. Test-retest reliability is fair on scales where the preference score was slight. There is some indication that one or more scales *may* be reported differently with a test-retest period of four years of college. Again, caution is necessary in utilizing old MBTI scores. Face to face interpretation is necessary to verify the results with the individual.

Other Settings

In the private practice of psychotherapy, I evaluate the appropriateness of MBTI administration on a case by case basis. I do not automatically administer the Indicator on the first visit. I first make an initial assessment of the client's needs. I follow the same approach when doing consultation, first making an assessment through interview and observation. Some practitioners use the MBTI for initial intake and information gathering, but my bias with all kinds of testing is to begin with face-to-face observation and interview.

APPROPRIATE USE OF THE MBTI

Counseling Goals

Once I have made an initial assessment of clients' needs and together we have formulated counseling goals, I will suggest use of the MBTI for the following kinds of issues and concerns:

- ∝ desire to explore career options and do life planning
- ∝ difficulty with a life/developmental passage or transition
- ∝ difficulty with interpersonal relationships and communications
- ∝ desire for self-exploration
- ∝ academic functioning and adjustment
- ∝ work functioning and performance
- ∝ leadership and organizational problems

The eighteen cases in the next chapter will illustrate most of these applications.

The MBTI has value beyond the specific kinds of issues and concerns just listed. Its use can enhance the counseling process by:

- ∝ developing a common vocabulary and concepts for working with clients and their concerns;
- ∝ validating client's perception of self;
- ∝ strengthening self-esteem and setting the direction for further self-development;
- ∝ providing an objective and concrete way to describe an emotionally loaded situation, such as a relationship conflict or work problem;
- ∝ offering a conceptual framework which aids clients to get a more objective view of themselves and their life situations, to view themselves from a fresh angle;
- ∝ suggesting specific language and approaches to use with individual clients to build rapport quickly and sustain a therapeutic relationship;
- ∝ pointing to possible areas of client difficulty as well as possible strengths;

∝ pointing to interventions that may be most appropriate for clients of different types;

Inappropriate Use of the MBTI

There are occasions when I don't believe the MBTI is appropriate. When the client is distrustful of therapists in general, of the counseling process, and of tests, use should be deferred. There should be some rapport and client trust before the MBTI is introduced. Some clients are not good candidates for the MBTI because they are too hyperactive to take the Indicator, are too disturbed, or are in acute crisis. Just as with other kinds of tests and inventories, the practitioner must use good judgment. If counselors sense any client reluctance to participate in testing, this reluctance should be explored before proceeding with test administration or interpretation. Inappropriate use, other than because of the psychological condition of the client, will be discussed later under "Ethics of Use."

INTRODUCING THE MBTI TO CLIENTS

When conditions are appropriate for using the MBTI, clients should be introduced to the Indicator in a way that makes sense to them in terms of their stated needs and the counseling goals. I explain what the MBTI can and cannot do. The MBTI is a tool for exploring personal strengths and preferences. It will not point to a specific choice or direction. The results are not so definitive or specific that any counseling issues will be "solved" by knowing one's type. A simple explanation can be given about how the results will relate to the agreed upon counseling goals. Examples are:

∝ in relationship counseling: "Knowing your preferences will help you to understand your style of communicating and how you may differ from your partner."

∝ in career counseling; "Understanding your preferences will help you to identify your strengths, how you might like to work, and what work settings might be satisfying to you."

∝ in academic counseling: "Your preferences will aid in identifying the ways you learn best as well as suggesting some learning skills you may wish to develop. We can use this information to formulate study approaches and choose appropriate academic courses."

∝ in counseling for mid-life transition: "Perhaps knowing your preferences will help us understand why you feel stuck at this point in your life and what you may need to feel satisfied."

Other important points to make with clients are:

∝ The MBTI is not a test; it is an indicator. There are no right or wrong answers.
∝ All preferences are equally valuable; there are no better types.
∝ The MBTI is based on normal human functioning and is not designed to measure psychopathology.
∝ The instrument has been in use for a long time, with good reliability and validity, established through many studies.

I also check for client questions about the MBTI and willingness to take it. Since the Indicator and *Manual* are both explicit about administration procedures, it is unnecessary to duplicate that information here. Most individual clients are given the question book and answer sheet to complete on their own at home. They are cautioned not to seek others' assistance in answering but to answer on their own in a non-distracting environment. The ideal, of course, is to have a quiet testing space at the counseling office. On occasion, I will require the client to complete the questions in my office if I suspect a poor test-taking environment at home. I tell clients who are tested individually that I will hand-score their answer sheets upon their next visit, since hand-scoring takes only about five minutes.

MBTI INTERPRETATION

At the time of interpretation, I begin with a restatement of what the MBTI results can and cannot do or reveal. I ask their reactions to answering the questions and give them an opportunity to express frustration at the forced-choice items. This is also an opportunity to check on whether there were any unusual test-taking conditions or attitudes. Clients are reminded of the limitations of all self reported inventories. The materials I use in interpretation vary but generally include:

∝ either the computer-scored printout or the hand-scoring report form.
∝ *"Verifying Your Type"* and *Introduction to Type*.
∝ depending on the depth of interpretation, other books such as *Gifts Differing*.

The language used in interpretation should be appropriate to the educational level and the type of the client. If a client prefers sensing, for example, a concrete, practical explanation will probably be more helpful than a theoretical one. Unbiased descriptions and careful avoidance of value-laden words are crucial. Counselors can monitor their

explanations and listen for biases or "favorites" implied in their interpretations. Sometimes clients get the impression that one preference is
more desirable than another. This impression can be corrected by asking the client for reaction or feedback. If clients seem disappointed
with the interpretation, counselors may have presented the preferences
in a biased fashion, or clients may have misunderstood explanations.
Since the MBTI is not one hundred percent accurate, a less than positive reaction may also signal that one or several of the preferences were
not accurately identified.

After explanation of the four dimensions, I demonstrate how the four
preferences combine to form one of sixteen possible types, illustrating
the dynamic aspects of type. Clients are asked their reactions to this
information. Results are then related to the ongoing counseling process
and goals. I might ask the client, "Does this have meaning for you in
relation to . . . ?" Finally, I may share my type with the client to promote
an atmosphere of equal-to-equal collaboration and to illustrate any differences. Mutual self-disclosure is usually helpful, but counselors should
use judgment about the appropriateness of sharing their types. The
same guidelines of self-disclosure for general counseling apply here.

Doubts About Type

Although individuals are usually consistent in how they report their
preferences whether they are answering from the perspective of their
work, their personal life, or some other setting, some clients question if
their results are their true type or merely the requirements or influences of a particular setting. These doubts can be explored to gain clarification about what is true type versus what may be required behavior
or desired performance. If exploration does not bring clarification, an
option is to have the client take the Indicator twice, once for each setting. I rarely use this option, since the counseling interview usually
uncovers the nature of the discrepancy in reported type. This confusion
seems to be more prevalent when preference scores are slight (score 1-
9). Slight preference scores mean clients "cast almost equal votes" for
both poles when they took the Indicator. It becomes very important to
clearly describe each pole with life examples so that the client can identify the actual preference. Sometimes individuals report slight preferences but upon reading the type description, are very clear that these
preferences fit for them. Sometimes slight preferences may indicate
some tension between the two poles. The tension could be the result of
a discrepancy between true preference and environmental demand or
press. An example is an ENFJ working in a large organization which is
predominantly ESTJ and ENTJ. This ENFJ client is unsure initially

about whether her preference is T or F. In processing her results, she identifies that her true nature is F, but she feels a strong pressure to act like a T on the job. Gender, family influences, and cultural differences are other factors that could possibly affect the way individuals answered the MBTI, contributing to possible doubts about the results.

When preference scores are slight, there are likely to be differences between the word pair section and the phrases section of the Indicator. The scores from these two sections are recorded on the administrative sheet of the computer-scored printout. If a client with a slight preference for T scores as an F on the word-pairs and as a T on the phrases, there may be some kind of tension (environmental or internal) in regard to this judgment function. The counselor can explore this possibility. Counselors who hand-score can mark their templates to delineate the items that are word pairs and phrases. Discrepancies between word pair and phrases should not be over-interpreted, however. If the client reads the type description and agrees with it, there is no need to probe further. There is still no conclusive research about the meaning of discrepancies between these two sections of the MBTI.

In summary, slight preference scores may mean:

∝ a period of transition and experimentation with both functions;
∝ a lack of development of that function, perhaps because of environmental factors;
∝ area of conflict, tension, or ambiguity;
∝ test-taking conditions such as instructions given and the setting.

Slight preferences may reflect different dynamics in middle or older aged adults compared to adolescents and young adults. The latter are likely to be crystallizing preferences, perhaps shedding parental influences. Older adults with slight preferences may be working under conditions which force them to operate against their types; may be undergoing a major lifestyle change, such as divorce; or may be consciously practicing using the opposite pole to their natural preference.

Counselors should never insist that a particular MBTI result "fits" a particular client. Sometimes clients are eager for closure and are frustrated by indeterminate, slight scores. SJs especially are likely to need suggestions as to specific steps they can take to determine their actual preferences. Some steps to clarify preferences are:

∝ Read other type descriptions of related types, to see if another description fits better.
∝ Within a type description, underline statements that seem true and put question marks where statements don't fit.

∝ Clients can show their type descriptions to several people who know them well and get feedback.
∝ Clients can be directed to observe specific behaviors such as how they make a decision.

This "homework" is then processed at a follow-up counseling session to further clarify actual preference. Clients should be supported for taking as much time as needed to learn about themselves and their preferences.

Over-Interpretation of Scores

Another caution about interpreting scores is not to assume because clients have clear preferences that they have proficient use of that particular preference. Nor should one assume conversely that very clear preferences indicate lack of ability to use the opposite pole. In other words, scores do not convey proficiency or excellence, or weakness. Counselors must remember that the MBTI is not a trait measuring instrument and so the MBTI scores are not handled in the same way. MBTI scores give counselors a confidence level about the clarity or certainty of the test-taker's preferences on the day of administration.

INTERPRETING THE MBTI TO DIFFERENT TYPES

My clinical experiences with the MBTI suggest varying the interpretation process somewhat to meet the needs of different types. Some of the more prominent differences are worth mentioning here. When working with clients with a preference for introversion, the interpretation process flows very differently than with extraverts. Introverts usually take in all the information about their type and ask few questions until they have had time to reflect on their results. They usually don't interrupt with questions and comments, as most extraverts are prone to do. Usually introverts appreciate some time to think about their results before asking questions or discussing personal relevance; therefore, a follow-up appointment for this purpose is recommended. Extraverts may move quickly into discussion of MBTI relevance to their lives, sometimes not allowing enough time to really consider the implications of the various dimensions. The Es may prefer a faster paced discussion. The counselor may need to pause more often and wait for introverted clients to formulate comments or questions. The counselor must take care to solicit feedback from introverted clients to make sure they understand. The Es will show signs of understanding or confusion more readily by their frequent responses.

Of course, the counselor's type is also a factor here. Extraverted counselors need to be careful to slow themselves down and allow enough pauses when working with introverted clients. Introverted counselors need to adjust to frequent interruptions from extraverted clients eager to interact about their results.

Another interpretation difference involves sensing and intuition. S types seem to prefer descriptive phrases and comments written down on the interpretive materials they are given. Examples from daily life are especially welcomed by Ss. I usually write out some sequential steps derived from their MBTI results. These steps might look like: (a) summary of ways client prefers to function, (b) potential career areas to explore, (c) first step to exploration (e.g. interview a person in the profession), (d) second step to exploration, and so forth. While many intuitives will ask about patterns, possibilities, and theory involved in the MBTI, Ss are generally more interested in the immediate applications. Many NPs like to apply the MBTI to career planning through brainstorming and divergent thinking, but the SJs usually become frustrated by divergent thinking. Usually SJs prefer convergence towards fewer options rather than expanding options. Good career counseling or counseling to solve problems includes both divergent and convergent stages, but the counselor will need to be sensitive to the tolerance levels for divergent and convergent thinking of the different types.

Another interesting difference is between thinking and feeling preferences. Often Ts will want data to substantiate implications of the Indicator. They may even ask about reliability and validity. Ts tend to he more skeptical about the instrument. If the counselor is an MBTI enthusiast, it is important not to brush off the T's skepticism, but rather to work with it by sharing information/data from the *Manual* and other MBTI materials as appropriate. Feeling types tend to become impatient with much data and are more likely to personalize results. An important distinction should be made in interpreting the meaning of the T-F scale. The counselor should be clear with the client that thinking preference does not mean clients don't have feelings, or vice versa, that Fs can't think logically. Rather, the counselor should stress that this scale is a reflection of two different rational processes, which use different criteria for making decisions/judgments. Ts place a higher priority on objective facts; Fs on interpersonal issues or subjective factors.

TYPE DIFFERENCES IN THE COUNSELING PROCESS

Establishing a Positive Counselor-Client Relationship

Therapists by being aware of their own types can monitor potential stylistic differences that could impede relationship building.

Because of their own type preferences, therapists may have their own blind spots or biases and may favor certain treatment approaches over others. A therapist's favorite approach might not match with a client whose type was very different. For example, one therapist with preferences for INFJ is very fond of bibliotherapy and assigns readings between sessions. One client who had ESFJ preferences terminated counseling with this therapist after two sessions because she felt put off by an attitude she perceived as "go read a book." What she wanted in therapy was an active interaction and place to talk out specific issues here and now.

Counselors can use understanding of type to build rapport with clients. Counselors are trained to "mirror" clients' body language, pacing, etc. Some therapeutic approaches such as Neurolinguistic Programming (NLP) particularly stress mirroring. By knowing client MBTI preferences, therapists can mirror those preferences to expedite counseling. Clients' MBTI preferences suggest to counselors specific language, phrasing, pacing, and examples to use. Counselors can learn to "talk 16 types." The following table gives some examples of ways of building the counselor-client relationship based on clients' MBTI preferences. Of course, other variables besides type account for client behavior, so this table can only reflect general tendencies.

BUILDING A HELPING RELATIONSHIP BY MATCHING CLIENTS' PREFERENCES

PACING OF INTERVENTION

EXTRAVERT	INTROVERT
Rapport—more "social chatter"	Rapport—go slowly, respecting natural reserve.
First step talking out loud for clarification.	Silences for reflection and crystalization before active talking.
Explaining through doing/action.	Explaining through written material or verbally with pauses for thought.
Rehearse, demonstrate, roleplay.	Encourage writing down questions and thoughts to share with helper.
Act expediently.	Prepare in advance for difficult procedures or interventions.

FOCUS OF UNDERSTANDING

SENSING	INTUITION
Give concrete specifics.	Give the broad view/big picture.
Economy of words; say it simply.	Allow dialogue about the concepts involved.
Give real life examples.	Use metaphors and look for connections.
Set realistic practical goals.	Set goals in broader terms allowing flexibility and variation.
Call upon common sense for problem solving.	Use imagination and novelty for problem solving.
Write down specific steps for change.	Keep the big goal in mind, like a map.
Support change through small incremental steps.	Support change through "giant" steps, or leaps of insight.

MOTIVATION FOR CHANGE

THINKING	FEELING
Show cause and effect of thoughts, actions and outcomes.	Examine the wholeness/gestalt of a situation.
Respect and respond to *"why."*	Respect and respond to affect and personal values.
Clearly show expertise as helper, including credentials.	Show personal interest and warmth.
Maintain a professional distance and intellectual authority.	Use personal stories of other helping experiences.
Present issues in logical terms.	Enter client's subjective experience or world.
Focus on developing skills, mastery, and competence.	Focus on personal values and and desired lifestyle.
Identify ways of measuring/evaluating improvement.	Identify ways of evaluating change based on values and relationships.

STYLE OF WORKING

JUDGMENT	PERCEPTION
Focus on outcome.	Focus on the process of helping
Offer a structure and "plan" (time limited).	Offer to be a "guide" or "coach" (not time limited).
Work towards closure.	Work in an open-ended way.

Although the table discusses separate dimensions of the MBTI, it is important to consider the type dynamics of the 16 types. For example, the suggestions for sensing would be particularly important if S were the dominant function and least important if the client were dominant intuitive.

Once counselors are fluent with type dynamics they begin instinctively to watch for behavior typical of specific types, forming hypotheses about clients' MBTI preferences. Many therapists use type concepts without administering the actual MBTI to clients. Sometimes counselors administer the MBTI later in the counseling relationship when it seems useful to make explicit type dynamics they have been working with implicitly. Although counselors can build rapport by mirroring clients' types, this does not mean that counselors should or can "become" the client's type. Counselors must be themselves and work from their own strengths. Talking a client's type is only the first step to reach the client. Next steps usually include challenging clients to develop and use other dimensions besides their natural preferences. Therapists work between the two poles of support and challenge. Merely talking the client's type will not necessarily solve a problem or encourage growth.

Client Expectations and Counseling Goals

Putting aside other variables such as age and multicultural factors, different types will approach counseling and the therapeutic process for different reasons and with differing expectations. Individuals with TJ preferences tend to view counselors as authorities or experts and therefore are likely to expect more active direction than other types. If in addition clients have preferences for S and/or E, these client attitudes are usually magnified. Very specific, time-limited problems are likely to bring them to counseling, not broad goals such as "to know myself better." These clients expect convergence on a solution and specific suggestions for how to deal with a problem; they want answers.

NPs, on the other hand, tend to look for a guide who will help them ask the important questions and "search" for new understandings and possible solutions. Although they may sometimes seek counseling because of an urgent problem, they are often motivated by broader goals of personal development or understanding. The NTs will usually gauge the value of counseling by the expertise of the therapist and will usually want to know about credentials and experience at the outset. In contrast, the NFs are more likely at the outset to gauge whether they are comfortable with the therapist and whether the therapist seems authentic and in solid "contact" with them. Fs in general are more concerned with the quality of caring shown by the therapist than by credentials and expertise. Obviously both sets of qualities are important, but different types will initially assess the value of counseling according to these differing criteria.

These are some of the ways types will vary. Consequently counseling goals which are mutually agreed upon by therapist and client can vary from brief therapy that is problem focused to open-ended insight work. The goals may be couched in quantitative, behavioral terms or in personal and abstract terms, depending on the language and preferences of clients. The cases in the next chapter are examples. In some of these cases, I identified other issues important to work on in counseling, but the client did not share the same interest, at least at that point. The discrepancies in desired counseling outcomes are explained in part by professional training but also by type differences between client and therapist. Therapists should be aware that their own types and their training lead them to have certain expectations about the nature of the counseling process, and that these expectations may be different from those of some of their clients. Negotiating these discrepancies is part of the counseling process and is most effective when the counselor is self-aware.

Choosing Appropriate Interventions

Some research (see Chapter Six) has already shown that therapists' types influence their preferred modalities or therapeutic approaches. Therapists can make the false assumptions that their preferred modalities are the most appropriate ones to use with their clients. Counselor education in recent years has stressed the importance of moving beyond ones preferred modality to a more flexible, eclectic approach that responds to the individual needs of clients. Type should be included in these considerations. The example was given earlier of an ESFJ client's poor response to bibliotherapy, favored by her INFJ therapist. Some other examples of modalities usually preferred are:

INTROVERSION	EXTRAVERSION
reading	talking
writing/journaling	role-playing
meditating, reflecting	rehearsing, practicing
individual therapy	group therapy

SENSING	INTUITION
behavioral therapy	insight therapy
skill-building demonstrations	imagery, active imagination
concrete directed homework	dreamwork
Reality Therapy	phenomenological, existential
hands-on experiences	reading

THINKING	FEELING
behavioral therapy	humanistic therapies
cognitive therapy	art therapy
problem-centered therapy	person-centered therapy

JUDGING	PERCEPTION
outcome-focused therapy	"search" or process-focus

The above list becomes modified by the interaction of the combined preferences, remembering again the importance of dominant and inferior functions. Other client variables may influence preferred therapy as well.

Counselors should start with interventions that engage the general strengths and the type strengths of the client. As mentioned previously, it is unwise to use an intervention early in the counseling process that engages the inferior function. After the relationship is on solid ground and the client is relatively stable may be a good time to use interventions to engage less preferred functions. By engaging the less preferred functions the therapist can help clients find more balance and develop other aspects of themselves. The following table gives examples:

HELPING CLIENTS DEVELOP BALANCE FOR GROWTH AND CHANGE

EXTRAVERT	INTROVERT
Interrupt talk, slow down rate of speech, encourage some silence for focusing on inner world/self.	Encourage verbal expression.
	Encourage confirming internal impressions with external "reality checks."
Encourage some reflection time in session and between sessions.	Encourage writing out questions and impressions and reading these out loud in sessions.

SENSING	INTUITION
Help to identify the pattern from all the details.	Encourage "grounding" through the senses.
Help to view situation from a new or different perspective.	Help to identify some specific and realistic steps.
	Encourage confirmation of hunches with concrete facts.

THINKING	FEELING
Encourage exploration in cause-and-effect terms. ("It is logical to feel this way because . . .")	Teach to analyze consequences.
Teach awareness of others or empathy. ("If you were in that situation, what do you think you would feel?")	Teach cause and effect thinking.
	Teach linkages between thoughts and emotions.

JUDGMENT	PERCEPTION
Encourage to gather more info before deciding.	Teach decision making strategies.
Stimulate playfulness and flexibility.	Teach self-management skills.
Encourage to suspend judgment and "just look" (stay open).	Teach goal-setting skills.

Attitudes Towards Change

In the section on mid-life in Chapter Two some of the attitudes different types have towards change were mentioned. Attitudes towards change affect the overall counseling process as well. Intuitive therapists are likely to conceive of change in terms of the big picture, looking into the future, patterns of lifestyle or behavioral shift. Sensing therapists may be more deliberate and sequential in the way they conceive change. Intuitives are likely to envision the destination and take giant steps to get there, even skip steps. Sensing types are likely to be acutely aware of what needs to be different in the moment and work carefully from there towards the future in small, incremental steps. These conditions are magnified if the N is also EN or ENP, and if the S is also IS or SJ.

Where client and counselor differ in their S-N preferences, the process can get deadlocked if the therapist is not aware of this difference. The S client can feel too rushed to change and threatened. The N client with an S therapist may become impatient and dissatisfied. Resistance and tension may emerge. The therapist can modify the counseling process and approach towards change to accommodate this difference. Respecting the client's orientation is essential, although that fine line always exists between support and challenge, so that the client's conception of change may need to be gently challenged at times.

MULTICULTURAL ISSUES IN USING THE MBTI

Sue (1981) states that culture "consists of all those things that people have learned to do, believe, value, and enjoy in their history. It is ideals, beliefs, skills, tools, customs, and institutions into which each member of society is born" (p37). For our discussion here, culture includes race, ethnicity, class, religion, gay-lesbian orientation, regional background, and all other such variables that contribute to the diversity of specific groups. Pedersen *et. al.* (1989) refer to a "cultural grid" composed of two dimensions. One dimension is composed of ethnographic, demographic, status, and affiliation variables which make up a person's social system. The other dimension is composed of personal cognitive variables of behavior, expectations and values (p36). MBTI preferences certainly are a part of this second dimension. Pedersen *et. al.* assert that within group (cultural) differences are greater than between group differences because of psychological characteristics. Therefore, the MBTI can help counselors understand individuals within a culturally different group.

Sue has observed that "attitudinal similarity" between counselor and client may be more important than racial similarity when connecting with the client. He adds that certain characteristics of the counselor may override race differences in the counseling relationship. Therefore, type similarities between counselor and client may compensate for cultural differences. In other words, type can be a bridge between counselors and clients who are different racially, ethnically, or in other ways. The literature of multicultural counseling compliments the literature of MBTI applications in counseling. Both literatures stress the importance of counselor sensitivity to and respect for differences and the necessity of mirroring client language, verbal and non-verbal. Pedersen *et. al.* assert, "Although counselors cannot change their cultural identity, they can learn the styles appropriate for working with culturally different clients and enhance the degree of perceived similarity between themselves and their clients" (p33). Both multicultural and type theories stress modifying the counseling process to meet the expectations, values, and styles of clients.

Type as a Bridge to the Client

Counselors and clients must connect in some way if counseling is to be helpful. If they share gender, class, sexual orientation, etc., they have some initial common ground. However, Sue and Pedersen have both cautioned against overlooking personal characteristics, which may affect the client-counselor relationship. There are many occasions when counselors and clients may be culturally different and yet share similar MBTI preferences. Here the MBTI can be the common ground. In yet other circumstances, counselors may be different from their clients both in culture and in type. Counselors who have developed the ability to "talk 16 types" can use this skill in bridging the differences. In many situations it may be easier or more effective for counselors to talk the client's type than to talk a particular ethnic "language." The following case illustrates this point.

A young Asian-American gay client sought counseling to improve his personal relationships with peers and his family. He lacked social skills and also was struggling with how and to whom to "come out." I differed in many ways from my client but did share dominant intuition. His preferences for INTJ suggested that he might be most comfortable with a counseling process that provided :

∝ initial discussion of my credentials and expertise.
∝ direct answers to his questions phrased in the language of "the expert."
∝ a systems model or framework for comprehending his relationship difficulties.
∝ within this systems model opportunity for him to select pieces to work on and practice with me at his own careful pace and then to place that piece back into the framework to see the whole.

Proceeding with the counseling process in this way readily built rapport and met his needs. Our work together spanned several years of episodic counseling. We both learned a lot from our relationship. Perhaps another counselor with extensive experience with Asian-American or gay culture would have used that experience as a "bridge," while I felt that a more feasible starting place for me was through my extensive experience working with INTJ clients.

Identity and Assimilation as Variables

A well-recognized model of assessing clients' cultural status is the two-way grid: degree of assimilation and degree of ethnic/cultural identity (Pedersen, *et. al.*). Clients who are highly assimilated blend into the predominant culture. They have embraced and are fluent with the language, values, etc. of the dominant culture. Individuals with high identity strongly identify with their cultural group in all respects—language, values, etc. Individuals who are high in both assimilation and identity are considered bicultural.

This model is a reminder to counselors that merely looking at the surface or obvious cultural differences of our clients does not inform us of their true nature. Two Chinese-Americans can be very different; one may be a highly assimilated third generation American while the other may have been born in China and have low assimilation. Clients' position on this grid affects type in two ways: one, how they react to taking the MBTI and two, how their types are expressed.

Caution should be used in administering and interpreting the MBTI to clients with low assimilation and high identity. These clients may have different reactions to testing procedures than the predominant culture. They may also have language difficulties in answering the MBTI questions accurately. They may have strong cultural injunctions about how they should be; sex role may be an especially important part of these injunctions. If there are strong injunctions, they may not agree with or be satisfied with their MBTI results. It may be difficult to ascertain true type. Cultural variables can "muddy the waters."

Several examples may be helpful here. I chaired a panel on cultural differences several years ago. An African-American psychologist Pat Battle presented her research suggesting that a disproportionate number of African-American young people were scoring as STJ. She challenged these results on the basis of interviews with this population and observations of how these individuals expressed themselves in their own communities. She proposed that there were far more Fs and Ps than actually reported. Another example are some Native American individuals raised on reservations and who took the MBTI. They've told me that their results, ISTJ and INTJ, were their "white-man's way to be." They reported difficulty in answering the questions because of the items themselves and awareness of discrepancies between their own culture and their needs to survive in a dominant and different culture. Perhaps the frequency of I, S, and T preferences reflects their reaction to stress, as suggested in the Ware and Rytting study mentioned in Chapter Two. Therefore, counselors should weigh the usefulness of administering the MBTI to clients with low assimilation and high identity. Sometimes the MBTI may be useful. Other times it may be more effective to use the concepts of the four dimensions either explicitly or implicitly without using the actual instrument.

The second way the two-way model affects using the MBTI is in the way assimilation and identity magnify or dampen the expression of the 16 types. I worked with a successful college student who was a first generation Cuban-American. She came out ENTP on the Indicator and confirmed this result. She did not, however, act like most other ENTPs I had known. She was more passive, more tentative in speaking out, and more influenced by tradition. We talked at length about the role of a Hispanic woman she was supposed to play in her culture and the incredible conflicts she experienced between her inner nature and her cultural environment. These conflicts were particularly painful when it came to her family. In her case, the MBTI was not only useful in helping her understand herself better and make life decisions, but also was a means to begin exploring her relationships with her family and her culture.

The ENTP woman is an example of the dampening effect of culture on type. The magnification effect can be seen in the case of an ISTJ first generation Asian-American woman. The characteristics of ISTJ were more pronounced than usually seen in this type. She was very reticent, literal, methodical, and deferential to authority figures. She was a challenging client for me to work with because of our cultural differences and our opposite types. Understanding type dynamics helped me modify my counseling approach to work with her. She probably would have been better served by a counselor with some natural common ground, though none was available at the time.

One last example of the interactive effects of culture and type is a young gay man with confirmed ENTJ preferences. In his academic work, he behaved as one would expect. He took a strong leadership role in the classroom; was very articulate in expressing his ideas; was competitive; set goals of mastery measured by grades, etc. In the rest of his lifestyle, however, he could be misread as an ENFP because of the influences of his gay community with which he was highly identified. Other young gay men I've worked with, who were still ambivalent about their sexual orientation and therefore did not have "high identity," did not demonstrate the same degree of interactive effects with their types.

Attitudes About the Counseling Process

Cultural differences affect perceptions about counseling. Clients will have differing expectations about the purpose of counseling and the role of the counselor. Some cultures stress respect for authority, so that clients from those cultures will expect counselors to behave as experts and authorities. They will expect the counselor to be active and directive. Clients from some cultural backgrounds will distrust "talk therapies." Some clients will be extremely ambivalent about being in counseling despite their difficulties because their culture says that people should "go to their own" when they have problems. Some cultures do not encourage the level of self-disclosure associated with Western psychotherapy. These are some of the many multicultural issues in counseling. It is not my purpose here to discuss approaches, since there is a whole body of literature on this.

My purpose here is to make the connection between these cultural influences and type. Again, there are issues of magnification or dampening of type attitudes towards counseling because of cultural background. The ISTJ Asian-American woman is a good example. ISTJs usually expect a more directive style of counseling than many other types and their world-view usually includes an ordered universe where there are authorities/experts and right and wrong answers. The combination of culture and type here make this particular client unusually deferential to the counselor. Points made earlier about type in the counseling process can be placed along side of multicultural considerations to give counselors a more thorough set of lenses for understanding their clients and their needs.

In Summary

The more lenses we use in attempting to understand our clients, the more effective our counseling is likely to be. Sue found that premature termination of counseling was at a rate of 50% for culturally different clients, compared to an anglo rate of 28%. By taking both culture and type into account, counselors are more likely to retain and help clients. Type can serve as a bridge to clients different from counselors. Type can also be a tool to explore tensions between clients and their cultures. When using the MBTI with culturally different clients, however, it is important to assess the degree of assimilation and identity.

ETHICS IN USING THE MBTI

All counselors and therapists have a code of ethics developed by their professions which include guidelines for ethical use of test materials. These ethics apply, of course, to using the MBTI. The Association of Psychological Type (APT) has a set of "Ethical Guidelines" specific to the MBTI adapted from the wisdom of other professional organizations.

The most obvious ethical issue is standardized administration. The MBTI should be used according to instructions on the booklet and in the *Manual*. This means, for instance, that specific questions should not be lifted from the Indicator to get a "quick reading" on a particular preference scale. It also means the instrument should be used on appropriate populations and results utilized as suggested in the *Manual.*

Confidentiality seems to have become more of an issue with the increased use of the MBTI. Results should be available only to clients unless they give permission for that information to be released to a third party. Often in the college setting, faculty, advisors, or others concerned about a student's welfare will ask about MBTI results. The confidential nature of results can be explained tactfully and the staff encouraged to discuss with the individual student their interest in learning MBTI results. Students may want to share their results with their advisors or others. In some cases, coaches and teachers have requested that their teams and classes sign a list to release their MBTI results. Since there could be subtle coercion involved, I discourage this approach. For example, it would be hard for a young student to refuse her coach's request to sign a release after the coach said the information would improve teamwork. My alternative to these requests is that coaches/teachers supply me with the names of those in the group interested in their results. Then I do a group interpretation and deliver results directly to each student. Activities can be structured in the group for sharing information related to teamwork, learning styles, or other issues. Students are in control of their results and the amount of information they choose to disclose. Coaches, teachers, or other staff involved with these groups are encouraged to share their types in these group activities, so a collaborative atmosphere is developed.

The confidentiality issue is a powerful one in private consulting as well. Employers have approached me about using the MBTI as a screening instrument for hiring and promotion. I have always declined and have tried to educate employers about a more constructive use of type information. The ethical and more effective use of the instrument occurs after the employee is functioning in an organization. Then type can be related to strengths, functions, team building, and professional development. When consulting with business groups, the same approach can be used as with student groups: a group explanation of MBTI and results given directly to the individuals, not to administrators or supervisors.

In addition to a general code of ethics for test use, a few other issues bear mentioning here. One is interpretive bias. Some users not thoroughly familiar with the MBTI or unaware of their own type biases may slant interpretation or send messages that a particular preference is "good" or less desireable. Another common misuse is over-generalizing results and implying that all people of a certain type behave the same way. Also important is assuring that accurate and sufficient information about results has been provided and that clients have had an opportunity to ask questions and clear up confusions. Short-hand labels and over-simplification to save time are misuses of the MBTI.

Finally, there are those awkward situations when a new MBTI enthusiast asks to take the MBTI question book home to administer to spouse, friend, roommate, etc. These enthusiasts are anxious to learn the type of their significant other and think they know enough to explain the results. The enthusiast does not have the skill to be objective and thorough in translating results. Also, this may become a power issue in a relationship. Some underlying coercion or some hidden agenda might be present. My response is to state my professional responsibility to give results directly to the individual tested; we arrange some way to do this.

These are some of the major ethical issues. Other "gray areas" will emerge for the practitioner. Counselors are encouraged to consult APT "Ethical Guidelines," their own profession's code of ethics, and colleagues to clarify gray areas. Attention to the ethics of MBTI use is crucial to safeguarding client rights and professionalism within counseling, therapy, and consultation.

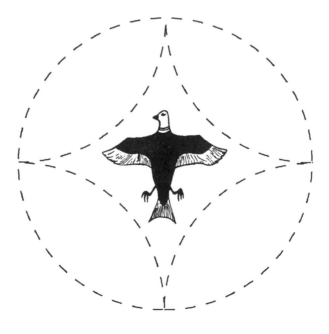

CHAPTER FOUR

Eighteen Cases

The core of this casebook is the clinical vignettes in this chapter. Eighteen cases have been chosen from my college and private counseling practices. Although client ages range from 18-45, a majority of the cases are young adults. Case selection was made on the following basis:

∝ to represent all 16 types and two other type conditions;
∝ to present personal problems typical for specific types;
∝ to include approximately equal numbers of men and women.

The cases describe the client's presenting problem and demonstrate how the MBTI was used in identifying the client's developmental needs, strengths and weaknesses. The cases also illustrate how the MBTI can help in formulating counseling goals and interventions. Although the cases chosen demonstrate the kinds of problems frequently seen in counseling for each type, one should not generalize that certain problems are inherent to certain types. Some cases represent brief therapy, one or two sessions in duration, and other cases reflect counseling contact over longer periods, up to several years. To keep cases brief and focused on MBTI applications in counseling, other counseling particulars unrelated to this casebook goal have been excluded. Counselors will know from their own practices that case descriptions do not capture all that transpires in their interactions with clients. Also, as reflected in actual practice, some of the clients described here were unwilling to commit to ongoing counseling and were looking for a "quick fix."

INTROVERTED INTUITION
with Feeling

INFJ

Dan—INFJ

Two "Personalities," One Career Decision

Dan was a sophomore referred by his academic advisor, who had sensed some emotional issues behind Dan's expressed interest in transferring to another college. Dan was uncomfortable mentioning the transfer, because this would be his third college within a two year period. He described his situation as a general "lack of motivation" to do his academic work. His analysis was that this particular college environment wasn't the "right one" for him and that when he found the right environment, he would "get motivated." In other words, Dan was looking for motivation from some external source. Dan had not chosen an academic major yet and had no career direction. He did feel strongly that he wanted to be in college at this time. He was bewildered about his lack of motivation and his paralysis in trying to make decisions about his future.

Dan felt much pressure from family members to major in something that would be "useful" and to make a career choice that would have high financial gain and status. He was the youngest of three brothers and felt a need to match their achievements. His father was a top executive with a prestigious corporation; his mother was a homemaker.

Dan's interests were vague. He thought he might like the social sciences but wasn't sure whether this was due to an older brother's influence. He liked a political science course he had taken and he liked to write.

After obtaining background information from Dan, we discussed the issues of motivation and decision making. He was able to articulate his need to establish a meaningful goal in his life. He chose to take two inventories to help with identifying a goal—the MBTI and the Strong Interest Inventory (SCII). During the next session we reviewed his MBTI results. Dan had clear preferences for INFJ. As we explored the meaning of these dimensions, he became much more animated and hopeful than previously. We spoke in general terms about career clusters that tended to appeal to INFJs (e.g. teaching, communications, counseling, writing) but planned to postpone focusing on specific occupations until after SCII results were also reviewed.

The SCII results, reviewed in the third session, were quite different from what one would usually expect for INFJ preferences. The SCII results also were not very congruent with statements Dan had made in the initial interview. Dan scored high on Conventional and Enterprising. The Conventional theme reflects desire for tradition, structure, office practice, defined tasks, and work in large, structured organizations. The Enterprising theme includes interests in leading, selling, persuading, public speaking, usually in business, public, or organizational settings.

I have found that INFJs and NFs in general usually score higher on the themes of Artistic and Social of the SCII. INFJs may occasionally score high on the Investigative theme as well. These differences between the MBTI and SCII, plus differences from interview information, suggested the possibility of internal conflicts and the need for further exploration. I have formed the opinion through years of utilizing these two inventories, that the MBTI will usually reflect the "truer" self, while the SCII may be more sensitive to external influences such as interests and values of significant others and role expectations. Therefore, counseling intervention focused on exploring incongruencies between self-reported conventional, structured interests and MBTI preferences for being creative, expressive, and individualistic.

This exploration provoked an animated response from Dan. He identified two "sides" of himself: "three-piece suit" and "true self" (his words). Three-piece suit represented his father's lifestyle—financial and social security, respectability, the adult male role. This was the only view of male adulthood he had been exposed to. In his upper middle class, suburban childhood every adult male on his block wore a three-piece suit, carried a briefcase, and worked as an executive in a large organization. He described his true self as not liking structure, creative, emotional, unexpressed, and "in hiding" from people, because people like his father wouldn't understand this self. Using a Gestalt Therapy approach, Dan was encouraged to create a dialogue between his two "sides." By playing out these two sides and verbalizing their respective attitudes, he was able to clarify thoughts and feelings associated with these two sides or polarities. He could then see how he had become "stuck" about school and careers. His true self was afraid to grow up if adulthood meant "three-piece suit, so he moved from school to school and avoided setting goals. Dan was metaphorically "dragging his feet" to slow down the process of movement toward adulthood. Yet he was unable to let go of the three-piece suit role because of its security and familiarity. Also as a clear feeling type, he feared family disapproval, especially his father's, if he did not pursue a three-piece suit career. It was very important to "belong" in his family and to please his parents.

Dan was torn by the pull of these polarities. Through several sessions utilizing Gestalt Therapy, he was able to integrate aspects of both poles and realize that he needed and could use aspects of both. Based on his expressed interests, test results, and discussion, several career areas emerged which Dan decided to explore: sports psychology/coaching and political science directed toward public administration. Sports psychology could utilize his NF preferences: empathy, desire to motivate people, creative solutions to complex human dynamics. This career field could also provide some structure, security, and status. Public administration might utilize his potential as a leader/manager and incorporate some of the values reflected in the SCII. INFJs tend to be sympathetic, conscientious, and organized.

Although our work together did not establish a final direction, it did free Dan up to begin moving forward. Energy that had been tied up in his internal struggle was now available for school and decision making. He became motivated. The MBTI was valuable in this case for quickly identifying unexpressed aspects of self and providing an objective structure and vocabulary for discussing this self. Reliance solely on an interest inventory for career and life planning would have given a false picture in which the true conflict would not have emerged. Dan did transfer to a larger university which had academic programs related to his interests in sports psychology and public administration. He planned to continue career and personal counseling there.

INTROVERTED FEELING
with Intuition

INFP

George—INFP

Unemployed Minister

George sought career counseling after being unemployed for a length of time. At mid-life he found himself discouraged and full of self-doubts. He wanted to "find a new direction" for his life. A personal history revealed the following:

∝ A multi-disciplinary undergraduate degree in political science, history, and social science;

∝ A master's degree from a divinity school;

∝ Several years in the military service during which he reported the most interesting work had been night time reconnaissance missions in Vietnam (because of the challenge, "need to be alert," surprise elements, and lack of structure);

∝ Earlier hopes of pursuing a career in missionary work thwarted because of health problems of a family member;

∝ Desire to have his own church but lack of success in obtaining a church appointment during the four years since graduating;

∝ Since graduate school, odd jobs such as building maintenance.

From George's history it became apparent that George had a serious conflict between his longing for a career in the church and his need to find a secure job. Because of his failure to find a job in the ministry, he wondered if he should retrain in some other career area, such as computers. After some reflection, George decided that he wasn't ready to give up his aspirations for work in the church, since he had felt "called by God," and this goal remained an important one for him.

I suggested he take the MBTI so that we would have a clearer idea of what his preferences and possible strengths were. I told him that research had been done with the MBTI and clergy. His results might suggest certain job functions and settings. MBTI results might also give us ideas on how to structure his job search. The MBTI is often a "check and balance" to information and perceptions derived from personal interviews. Where discrepancies emerge between results and reported interests, strengths, etc., further exploration of these areas should he done. Where there is substantial agreement between results and the interview, the client feels validated. George agreed to take the MBTI and return for a second, interpretive session.

George reported very clear preferences for INFP. The preferences were explained to him in detail using examples drawn from interview information of the previous session and showing career applications for each dimension. Some examples of his INFP preferences were:

∝ His diverse interest in academic subjects as an undergraduate and his difficulty in focusing on any one academic major (INP);
∝ His penchant for digressing during the sessions into discussions of patterns and trends in religious thinking; he loved theory and new ideas (N). I pointed out to him that he had preferences similar to those of many college professors and others working in an academic environment;
∝ His unwillingness to compromise his strong religious and personal beliefs in terms of the type of church he was willing to serve (F);
∝ These beliefs were adhered to even in the face of "hard, cold economic facts" and practicalities (dominant F);
∝ His lack of persistence in the job search, lack of enterprising behavior necessary to find a job, and his turning inward in discouragement. He was stuck or paralyzed at this point in his life (IP).

Often when INFPs and INTPs become thwarted, they do not persist. They may change their original goals rather than struggle against obstacles.

This last characteristic was thoroughly explored with George so that he could understand and express feelings related to his current situation. Ways of confronting obstacles and persisting, instead of withdrawing, were discussed. One suggestion was to act "out-of-character" by designing a weekly plan of job search activities with specific tasks for each day. He must complete these activities in a "professional" manner. As an INFP, he was likely to put off job search efforts and wait for something to "fall into his lap." Also, negative responses from prospective employers could send George back into discouraged withdrawal unless he had promised himself to follow his "professional" plan day by day. He was encouraged to hold before himself the image of the goal he was seeking in the church. When he became discouraged, he could picture this image (taking advantage of his visual orientation, frequent in NFs). INFPs can persist when the goal is personally meaningful and well-defined.

The next step in counseling focused on work settings, job functions, resumes, and how to talk about his strengths in interviews using the MBTI information. Together we made a list of some of George's strengths which would be important in his work:

∝ ability to listen and consider thoroughly and empathically (INP);
∝ patience with theory and love of complexity (IN);
∝ imagination and creativity (N);
∝ ability to see patterns and possibilities in people situations (NF);
∝ quiet warmth and caring (IF);
∝ strong faith and belief in values (NF);
∝ flexibility (P).

Pastoral counseling emerged as a strong interest; a large percentage of INFPs are attracted to counseling. Other interests were campus ministry, editing religious publications, work in religious publishing houses, and Christian education. George also planned to pursue more systematically the possibility of his own church. We discussed his possible avoidance of fundraising and "nitty-gritty" budget management aspects of having his own church. He might want to examine a prospective church to see if others on the church staff could fill these functions leaving him free to do what he did best. George could also emphasize in church interviews that his strengths were in preaching, teaching, and counseling (as opposed to fundraising and organization). We brainstormed a list of contacts and potential employers. At the end of the session George said he planned to throw himself into these job search efforts and would get back with me if he found himself discouraged or stuck. He realized there was much for him to do and was challenged by this.

The MBTI was especially helpful in validating George's strengths at a time in mid-life when he experienced great self-doubt and discouragement. He was helped to understand the intrapersonal dynamics which prevented him from meeting his goals and learned some ways of overcoming or changing his way of coping. He left these two sessions with a more positive outlook and improved self-esteem. This was a case of brief therapy with no further contact, although George was encouraged to continue counseling if he met with any difficulties.

INTROVERTED ?
with Intuition

INxP

Carol—INxP

The Inability to Evaluate

Carol was a 40 year old divorced woman who sought counseling for her depression and confusion. She described her depression as an overwhelming sense of discouragement and helplessness about facing decisions and dealing with life. Carol felt paralyzed, in "a fog," unable to discern what was real from her inner conceptualizations. Carol added that she wasn't in touch with her "true self. " She stated that different people saw different images of her, leading her to wonder if there was one true image/self.

The MBTI was suggested as one of the counseling tools that could aid her in getting in touch with her true self and secondarily aid her in making impending lifestyle choices (career change, relocation, etc.). Her results, INxP, were clear preferences on all dimensions except Thinking-Feeling, where she scored F1.

Her auxiliary function, intuition, was well-developed. As an Introvert, she used her auxiliary function to interact with the outer world. In fact, she had developed intuition to such an extent that she was regarded as an extremely gifted student and creative writer. Many viewed her as someone with a quick grasp for concepts, intellectual, and imaginative. Her strong intuition, however, led her to perceive every issue as complex and multi-faceted. No decision or event could be interpreted simply; Carol often tied herself up in mental knots. There was no balance of intuition with thinking or feeling; her dominant function was not developed.

Thinking or feeling should have been her dominant function based

44

on the INxP combination. Yet her score on this dimension was in the middle. Introverts use their dominant function within themselves, as opposed to with the external world. Consequently, introverts may develop their auxiliaries before their dominant functions, since they need a tool for interacting with the environment. The judgment function when introverted often seems more slow to develop. Her scores echoed inhibitions of her type development due to her environment. She had a miserable and bizarre childhood, impacted by an alcoholic parent. At a very early age, she had resorted to daydreaming, fantasizing, and looking at bitter realities from novel or humorous angles. She had worked hard to avoid evaluating her reactions or making contact with her feelings about her family. Finally, she had been so good at using intuition as a child in school, that she had received external rewards and recognition which reinforced this preference.

One of the goals of therapy, in terms of an MBTI framework, was to help her learn to access her evaluative or judging function and develop either thinking or feeling. In developing this function, she would get a better sense of self by having a way to evaluate outside stimuli, possibilities, events in relation to her internal "self" criteria.

These counseling issues were explored with the client over several sessions. One of the counseling goals we agreed upon was to learn to access one of the judgment functions and experiment with this. Interventions were chosen to facilitate her going inside and practicing using both thinking and feeling. To practice thinking, Carol would have to examine consequences of choices/actions and weigh the merits analytically and objectively. To practice feeling she would have to ask herself, "What do I value? What's important to me? What do I care about most?" My approach drew primarily from Gestalt Therapy and values clarification techniques. Other helpful modalities were a system Gendlin (1981) developed called "focusing," meditation, and guided imagery.

For example, Carol would be asked to suspend talking and internal "chatter" to search deep inside herself for some place of awareness or "knowing." She was encouraged to use simple descriptive words to observe sensory impressions and body awareness. She was discouraged and interrupted from shifting to intuitive speculation and theorizing. Carol had to exert much effort to be aware of herself in an immediate, sensory way. Her process was that as she got close to an emotion, she immediately skirted it, rushing back to her "head." Coping with intuition was so well established that she continuously attempted to shift back to that mode. Therapy required gentle but firm persistence and redirection to practice using her other functions.

Values clarification techniques were utilized to help her identify her values, how they were shaped, and how to employ her values as criteria in making judgments.

Meditation approaches were particularly helpful, because these assisted her to go inside and get in touch with her physical and spiritual selves. She was instructed in deep breathing and relaxation exercises. Guided imagery was occasionally added, such as imagining climbing a mountain and meeting a wise being who spoke to her. The guided imagery harnessed her intuition in the service of accessing thinking or feeling.

Through several months of weekly sessions, she explored her inner self and her evaluative process. She began to identify with the feeling function and to learn how to access that function. She realized how she often "protected" herself from experiencing pain or discomfort by shifting to intuition. She felt a "split" in the past between her "head," and her "body" but now began to experience herself as a "whole solid self."

This new self-awareness of her process was then applied to impending life decisions. Although she still was somewhat uncomfortable making decisions, she felt more confident in making them with her newly discovered judgment function, feeling. By using techniques and processes learned in counseling, she now knew how to get in touch with her inner nature/needs/values to sort out choices that were appropriate for her. She found herself with more energy, and the depression lifted. Long after our counseling relationship was terminated, she wrote to say she had made several important life decisions—marriage, career, and relocation. Her letter reflected her positive outlook.

EXTRAVERTED INTUITION
with Feeling

ENFP

N

T

Toni—ENFP

Playing Versus Achievement

The scoring printout from CAPT says in its final paragraph about the ENFP:

If their judgment is undeveloped, they may commit themselves to ill-chosen projects, fail to finish anything, and squander their inspirations, abilities, and energy on irrelevant, half-done jobs. At their worst, they are unstable, undependable, fickle, and easily discouraged.

This cautionary statement applies to a number of the young adult ENFPs with whom I've worked. When their auxiliary, F, is undeveloped, these individuals may appear to be "busy bees" or "social butterflies," extending themselves way beyond their physical limits and often developing stress-related illnesses or exhaustion. Sometimes they exhibit hysterical behavior when they are not grounded and balanced by developed judgment. Mood swings may also be a problem; periods of overextension are followed by exhaustion and discouragement. In contrast, ENFPs with a developed balancing function, F, are usually energetic and involved, but usually keep activities at a manageable level. They are more likely to introvert periodically so they can use their feeling to sort through all the choices and activities.

Toni is an example of an ENFP with undeveloped judgment. Toni sought counseling near the end of her freshman year in college. She was doing poorly in her pre-med classes. She felt unmotivated to study and guilty about this. She admitted to an extremely active social life involving drinking, smoking pot, and late partying on school nights. She was a whirlwind of social activity. She was also concerned about her deteriorating relationship with her family. Initial counseling goals were to help her to clarify her present situation, to express related feel-

47

ings, to learn to manage her time, and to achieve a better balance between academics and social life. The MBTI was introduced as a way to look at her learning style and preferences, which might illuminate the way she was coping with college life. Her MBTI results were available from freshman class testing. We reviewed these results during the second session. Dimensions were described thoroughly with their implications for learning, studying approaches, academic strengths, and potential weaker areas. She had clear preferences for ENP, and a mild preference for F.

Toni lacked awareness of her inner process and its influence on her behavior. A Gestalt approach was employed to heighten her awareness. For example, she was asked to imagine her mother present in the room and to talk with her about their current conflict. As feelings emerged, Toni was assisted in identifying these and exploring them further. Her auxiliary F was not well-developed so she had not learned to suspend external activity to introvert and listen to her feeling judgment. The Gestalt approach was a way to coach her in developing her F. This approach also appealed to her ENFP preference for experiential methods.

Through an imagined dialogue with her mother, Toni also became aware that she had a strong conflict or tension between two poles which she identified as "the achiever" and "the player." On the one hand, she was stimulated and excited about the sciences and learning in general. On the other hand, she rebelled against structure, organization, the "have-to's" of homework. She wanted a playful, free-spirited existence, as do many EP types. My role was to help her understand these two sides of herself and how this tension between the two impacted her daily life. In Gestalt theory the individual works towards integration of elements of both poles, since both poles represent vital elements of the self. She was encouraged to use her feeling function to evaluate what was really important to her. In addition to Gestalt approaches, such as dialogue between her playful and achieving selves, she was encouraged to find daily quiet time "to go inside" and to keep a stream-of-consciousness journal. Journal writing may not always come naturally to young extraverts, but is a good way to slow them down to use their other introverted functions.

At this early point in our work together, she was not ready to take responsibility for her choices and behaviors. It was also apparent that she needed continuing counseling to assist in development of her auxiliary function. Over a period of months, she vacillated between wanting to change her lifestyle and resisting taking charge. She blamed circumstances, her friends, and family. Toni felt buffeted by fate and "controlled" by time. I challenged her to identity her own feelings and needs and evaluate behaviors on that basis; in other words, to take charge instead of just reacting. Many clients with a P preference resist closure and decision making and may even displace the responsibility for decisions to "fate."

Toni blamed her friends for not being able to say no to requests or invitations. Often feeling types have this difficulty because of the need for harmony and approval. We worked on assertiveness techniques for saying no. She practiced using her auxiliary to answer the questions: "What is it I need at this moment? What is important to me?" As with most NFs, relationships were of prime importance to her. If her relationships weren't going well, schoolwork seemed inconsequential to her. She needed assertiveness and interpersonal skills to help her achieve balance in her life. When her relationships were more satisfying, she concentrated on her studies.

During the first few months in counseling, Toni's academic performance was up and down. She would express intentions of getting organized, work with a burst of energy, then avoid work, socialize and party to exhaustion. Toni, like other ENFPs without well-developed feeling judgment, had initial bursts of enthusiasm and energy for her courses and assignments but then did not follow through. We continued to work on issues of setting priorities, taking responsibility for her behavior, and taking control of her own life. She did not need techniques on how to organize herself and on how to study; she knew how. What defeated her periodically was her own inner conflict and the lack of commitment to use this knowledge. Thus, counseling interventions continued to be directed towards these internal conflicts and empowering her judgment function.

These interventions gradually led to improved use of her feeling function, better understanding of herself, and a more balanced lifestyle. Toni changed her major to English and felt more satisfied with herself and her school performance. She loved literature and writing and was better able to sustain academic interest than in the sciences. She also felt that she wouldn't have to sacrifice her important relationships with this major, as she would in pre-med. Understanding her preferences for ENFP suggested the above counseling approach and a plan for personal development. I lost contact with Toni following her successful completion of college.

INTROVERTED SENSING with FEELING

ISFJ

Jesse—ISFJ

A Struggle for Independence

Jesse exemplified the young client who is nonassertive and struggling with dependency issues. Many ISFJ clients, usually young but sometimes at mid-life, have these concerns. Such clients usually engage in long-term counseling. Therapists must guard against fostering dependency while they are working to help these clients develop their autonomy.

Jesse sought counseling early in her college career because she felt depressed. She was a slow learner by her own definition, and was working very hard just to earn C's. She had difficulty grasping abstract concepts, an essential requirement of most of her college courses. She had not become involved with her peers. Jesse was the youngest of three, the "baby" of the family, and still dependent on other family members for decision making. She was impatient with herself and with any sort of complexity (in academic or life situations). Jesse saw herself as "dumb." She took herself very seriously, with little sense of humor or ability to get outside herself and get another perspective.

Jesse expected me to give her specific directions or "how-to's" for coping with college. She became confused when I was non-directive and also when I shifted from her focus on concrete daily problems to exploration of the patterns of her coping. She did not relate to metaphors or imagery activities. Furthermore, Jesse had difficulty generalizing a specific piece of learning in a given situation to other situations. As an ENFP, I had to change my approach to be more structured and concrete, so that I could "join" with her and not leave her confused because our styles were so different.

Jesse had very clear preferences for ISFJ. These results were interpreted to explore and affirm her potential strengths and to formulate counseling strategies to help her academic adjustment. Some of her strengths for coping in college were: conscientiousness (ISJ), caring and personal warmth (F), persistence and organization (J). Mutually agreed upon goals were to use the strengths of her preferences and also to develop her less-preferred functions. Counseling sessions were structured with these specific goals, mutually established:

∝ to develop other learning strategies to handle college courses;
∝ to work towards independence and making her own decisions;
∝ to learn assertive behavior;
∝ to become more playful and flexible.

The learning approach natural to most ISFJs was discussed along with discussion of other learning approaches necessary to handle college work. As an ISFJ, she was deliberate, thorough, and therefore often slower than many other types. ISFJs are often slower readers, focusing on one word at a time. Reading skills development for them includes teaching them to scan and group words to increase speed. Jesse also preferred learning in a hands-on (S), practical (S), personal (F), linear (S) and structured (J) way. Almost all of her professors preferred N, and most were NT. (Many faculty had taken the MBTI as part of a workshop.) Differences in teaching and learning styles were discussed. The N professors generally taught in a global, non-sequential way, sometimes without showing how theories and ideas were connected. An S student usually prefers to learn by building to a theory with step-by-step information (linear approach). An N student prefers to learn by seeing the theory or "big picture" first and then several examples to illustrate the theory (global approach). Ss often become frustrated with global teachers who jump from concept to concept. Ns often become bored with teachers who are deliberate and systematic in presenting detailed information. Her thinking professors were generally more impersonal than Jesse liked and was used to in the past. Although she would continue to favor learning with sensing and feeling, she could develop the ability to utilize her intuition for abstraction and her thinking for analysis. Plans were made for her to attend the Learning Skills Center to improve reading speed, comprehension, and study skills. Jesse was encouraged to see herself as not less intelligent than others but rather in need of different ways to learn in college.

ISFJs often have difficulty saying no to people's requests and are very concerned about harmony. Furthermore, they may have a tendency to internalize anger. These characteristics are strong factors in many of the depressed ISFJ clients I see, particularly female clients, who generally are more socialized to internalize anger. Jesse usually took the blame or responsibility for any interpersonal conflict and rarely expressed angry or hurt feelings. Assertiveness training through individual and later group counseling developed her communication skills in these areas. These skills helped her to assert herself with family, and she began to make her own decisions. Change was very gradual, since Jesse was apprehensive about change and not willing to take risks. She held on to the old and familiar.

In regard to change, if I pushed her too quickly or too hard to try a new behavior, she would resist and cling to the old way more determinedly. ISJ types may respond this way to change oriented therapists. Our relationship was a series of gentle pushes, cautious tries, and sometimes retreats. Occasionally I would take the other tack and suggest, paradoxically, that she wasn't "ready" for a particular change and should be "more cautious," "go slower." Then Jesse's response was to move forward without resisting the suggestion. Most difficult for her was accessing her playful, spontaneous "child" within. She was safer with carefully structured and serious activities. Yet she described her life as dull and devoid of fun. As she developed more trust in me and more faith in herself to try new behaviors, I was able to coax her into more playful behaviors. Being encouraged to exaggerate a rigid behavior during a session helped her to learn to laugh at herself. Another approach was to ask her to describe a time in childhood when she was mischievous or had fun. The description was used to help her access past playful feelings. Sometimes we playfully brainstormed "out-of-character" things she could do. Then her homework was to try one of these things and note her reaction and reactions of others to her. Again, Jesse always needed some kind of structure for her growth and the counseling sessions.

In helping her develop her intuition to see the broader patterns of her behaviors, I used very concrete metaphors at first, such as driving a car. Shifting gears was analogous to adapting, and the gears were MBTI functions. Over a period of several years, Jesse gained insight into herself and her coping patterns.

Sessions spanned several years but were not continuous. Rather, particular issues were worked on, followed by time away from counseling to practice new learnings. This periodic counseling prevented intense dependency on me. She became depressed much less often and less severely and recognized when she was being impatient with herself. I also learned from Jesse to be more patient. Her way of growing and changing was very different from what I naturally preferred. Mutual respect and fascination with each other's processes were important elements in our counseling relationship.

There is positive postscript. Jesse called me long after graduation to share her enthusiasm about her elementary teaching job. She was living on her own and feeling quite confident and competent. She described several teaching incidents where she had used her other functions to work creatively and flexibly with the children. And she said, "I'm starting back to graduate school part time!"

The Roommate Conflict—ISFJ vs. ENFP

The resident aide in the dormitory had tried to resolve emerging conflicts between two freshman women. When the conflicts continued, she referred the students to me. They came in together and expressed an interest in resolving the tension caused by their differences. They said they basically liked and enjoyed each other and wanted to stay friends, but their differences in values and lifestyles were getting in the way. They wanted me to arbitrate, to say who was "right" and who was "wrong."

The ISFJ (Mary) was the more upset of the two. She complained that Lana (ENFP) was giving their room and consequently herself a bad reputation by bringing "lots of guys" to the room. Mary felt judged by others in the living unit for associating with someone labeled by some others as "loose." Although she wanted to do things with Lana, she was reluctant because of this issue. She called herself an "old-fashioned" person who believed in dating one person at a time and reserving sexual intimacy for marriage. Furthermore, she felt thrown off balance when Lana invited friends without telling her in advance. Mary had a strong belief that the room should be a place of refuge and security. She could not understand Lana's behavior.

Lana, on the other hand, expressed hurt feelings and frustration at not being accepted by Mary. She said she was willing to accept Mary as she was, but felt as if Mary was trying to "impose her moral values" and social style on Lana. Lana's attitude was, "everyone should do their own thing."

After initial exploration of their perceptions of the problem, we began to examine differences using the MBTI, which all freshmen took during orientation. The MBTI was presented as a tool to look at differences in preferences for how individuals looked at situations and evaluated them. The MBTI might also help them understand some lifestyle differences. Through understanding these differences they might come to appreciate the strengths each had to offer the other and realize that many of the conflicts were not deliberately directed at each other but were rather an expression of their preferences. Each dimension was explained, with specific references and examples related to their conflicts.

Some of the most relevant aspects of differences revealed by the MBTI scales and discussed with Mary and Lana were:

∝ **Introvert (I)—Extravert (E):** Mary (I) needed quiet space and sanctuary from college activity. She had a lower tolerance than Lana for having many visitors to the room. Lana preferred many social contacts and had a lower need for privacy than Mary.

∝ **Sensing (S)—Intuition (N):** Mary (S) held strong traditional views and was initially unable to see other possible value systems or to see the world through Lana's eyes. Lana, with her intuition, challenged traditional views and looked for new possibilities in lifestyle and friendships. Lana could not accept "black and white" views.

∝ **Thinking (T)—Feeling (F):** The only dimension on which both had the same preference. Their preference for Feeling was evident in the efforts of both to express their personal values and reactions. This commonality was underscored and much validation given for the efforts and openness both displayed in dealing with the conflict. Also underscored was the mutually held motivation to enhance the friendship.

∝ **Judgment (J)—Perception (P):** Mary's preference for judgment was reflected in her need for more structure and security. She wanted to know in advance when Lana brought a boyfriend to the room. She wanted the use of the room (sleeping, socializing, etc.) to be more planned out and to feel in control of these issues. Lana, on the other hand, with a preference for perception, disliked setting a specific plan for their living space. She preferred spontaneous activity and variety from day to day. Furthermore, she tended to be less orderly in housekeeping than Mary.

This discussion helped Mary and Lana clarify some of their needs in relation to the living situation:

∝ Mary's needs: sanctuary, privacy, security, a "good" image among peers.

∝ Lana's needs: freedom, individuality, non-conformity, understanding and acceptance.

55

Mary and Lana were then able to move beyond the stuck point of "I can't understand why you do this" to seeing clearly that there were strong individual differences in style and values. Mary might not be able to grasp Lana's perspective, but she could accept the differences described by the MBTI. Lana gained a new appreciation for Mary's difficulty in living with Lana's way of doing things.

Moving from insight to action, each was first asked to restate what she saw as the basic differences in style, values, and needs.

Each gave the other feedback on the accuracy of these statements. Their perceptions had become more objective, less personalized, and less emotional. With a more objective viewpoint they were better able to see actions they could take to make things better.

At the end of this session, they were presented with a decision to consider for discussion at our next appointment. There were clear personality differences which had been and could continue to be a source of conflict. These differences had nothing to do with the qualities of each as a person. They could choose to find new roommates, or they could choose to work on these differences. In the latter case, the basic differences could provide excitement and a growth experience for both. This could be a complementary relationship, where each could benefit from the strengths of the other (e.g., Mary could provide a sense of stability; Lana could introduce new experiences).

Lana and Mary chose to remain roommates because they both valued the friendship and felt confident in their abilities to communicate with each other. With coaching, they worked through some basic issues of daily living, compromising to meet each other's needs. Examples of some of the compromises and ground rules established were:

∝ Lana would check with Mary before bringing young men to the room.
∝ Mary would not "preach" to Lana about her dating behaviors.
∝ Lana would find other locations for socializing besides their room.

None of these compromises was forced but were carefully thought through and volunteered by Mary and Lana. Communications skills were taught using a behavioral model similar to that used in couples counseling.

Finally, they were asked to return in several weeks to let me know how things were going. At that follow-up and again three months later, they reported reduced tension and increased satisfaction with each other as roommates. They were able to view themselves and their differences with good humor.

INTROVERTED SENSING
with Thinking

ISTJ

Jeri—ISTJ

Resistance to Change

Jeri's process was much like Jesse's (ISFJ). The dominant function for both was introverted sensing. Jeri's case will illustrate several additional aspects of this related type. Jeri came to see me because of stress and worries about not getting "all A's" her first term in college. She appeared anxious and reported feeling "tight" with frequent "tension headaches." She had set an " all A's" standard for herself and was now angry with the system (teachers, methods of evaluation) and herself for not meeting this standard. Jeri was a perfectionist in all areas of her life: appearance, eating behaviors, social and academic performance. For example, her naturally curly hair was a preoccupation with her since she couldn't "control" it. She determinedly subdued her hair with pomade and a tight braid—a metaphor for how she treated herself. In her friendships she had rigid expectations of how her girlfriends should act, when they should call, etc.

Although she expressed unhappiness at her stress level, she was unwilling to examine her underlying beliefs, standards, and coping style. What she wanted from me was a formula for how to achieve her original goal of all A's. The counseling process was described to her as one of working together to sort out problems and find alternatives. There was no formula or set of directions I could give her that would relieve her anxiety. Jeri was obsessive-compulsive, strongly defended, and reluctant to question or modify any of these defenses. Not only was she resistant to change, but our complete opposite MBTI types added to differences in how we viewed change. I saw that even a gentle nudge caused her to hold on even more tightly to established beliefs and coping patterns.

I did not discuss Jeri's MBTI results with her, although I had looked up her results (from freshman testing) before our session. When clients are defended and anxious, it may be inappropriate and non-therapeutic to use the MBTI. Jeri might have shut down further or become more anxious about whether she was the "right" type, and so on. Instead, I used her type information to guide my approach, keeping in mind that Jeri and I had not actually verified that ISTJ was accurate for her. Without this verification, ISTJ was only a working hypothesis.

Starting with where she was became essential to any counseling progress. This meant trying to see the world through her ISTJ eyes and to use her "language" (vocabulary and phrasing). Together we examined her study techniques. Her approach was concrete and rote. She overstudied by rereading material several times, trying to memorize everything. Although this approach had worked in high school, it unfortunately did not work well with abstract, college level course material, which required a higher level of learning (analysis and synthesis). She had difficulty particularly with essay tests and term papers. We discussed linear and global learning styles without my explicitly mentioning her sensing preference. Her preference was to learn in a linear, sequential, step-by-step way. Many of her courses necessitated global, non-sequential, concept-linking learning. Suggestions were made for new study approaches, and referral was made to the study skills center. Jeri was reluctant to let go of her old ways to try new approaches. She believed that "more of the same" or "just working harder" would produce the A's. She was, therefore, not very receptive to help from the skills center.

Counseling goals with Jeri were limited. She achieved some relief from her stress and frustration by being able to ventilate feelings and receive support, but she was not ready to modify her approach. She continued to insist on results (A's) and remained frustrated with the "system" and herself. Her tension headaches continued despite several sessions devoted to stress reduction through exercise and muscle relaxation. She decided that all her problems were physical. Consequently she persuaded her family doctor to write a prescription for valium. Jeri then informed me that she felt counseling was no longer necessary since her family doctor was now "treating" her.

Her behavior was consistent with her initial expectations that counseling should be "giving me the solution." While conveying respect for her right to choose valium as a way to control stress, I urged her to consider further counseling with me or someone not affiliated with the college. I voiced my personal concern that she look for other ways to deal with stress and consider my willingness to work with her in the future. In the last session we explored the possibility of Jeri taking time off from school. The grading system of college magnified her perfectionistic strivings. Another environment, other than school, might allow her to grow and loosen her defenses. Jeri did, in fact, take a leave of absence from college at the end of her freshman year and took a job. There was no way to know whether she sought further counseling after leaving.

Since Jeri was obsessive compulsive, her behaviors were much more exaggerated than that of other ISTJs I've observed clinically.

Many other ISTJs have reacted to counseling in a similar though less extreme fashion: a preference for concrete, structured outcomes in counseling (such as a pill) and discomfort with probing inner motivations and feelings. Mature ISTJs, who are in the process of developing their third and fourth functions (F and N respectively), are usually more amenable to insight or growth therapy. Perhaps a counselor close in type to Jeri would have been more effective. Jung talked about the benefits of pairing therapist and client of similar types to lessen the gap in behavioral modeling.

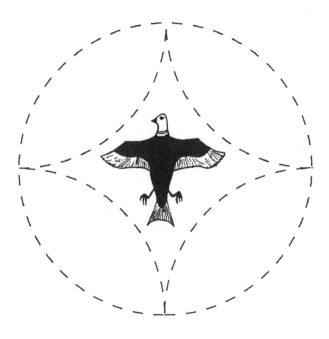

N
T
𝓕
S

INTROVERTED INTUITION
with Thinking

INTJ

Wendel—INTJ—In Pursuit of Utopia

Wendel came to see me in Spring of his freshman year in college, because he felt unmotivated about school and lacked career direction. Interviewing revealed strong interests in nutrition, the outdoors, and athletics. His MBTI showed preferences for INTJ, verified by him. His type tempered how he expressed these interests. For example, his interest in nutrition was directed to accurate, scientific knowledge that would link what one ate with physical fitness. The outdoors, to Wendel, was a political battleground; his idealism about nature challenged the pollution and misuse of the land by modern technology. His involvement in athletics was in terms of individual mastery (NT). He set extremely high standards for himself and for his environment (NT, especially INTJ). With his critical eye, no element of his surrounding environment met these standards. Furthermore, he was disappointed in himself for not meeting his standards (grades, athletic achievement, etc.). Wendel had a lot of "shoulds."

Many of the young INTJs I have known are as intense and self-critical as Wendel. They are preoccupied with principles and mastery and often frustrated at not finding a personal system and an environmental system to satisfy their standards. Even in mid-life some of these frustrations may still exist.

His freshman MBTI results were discussed in relation to these personal issues and to career possibilities. Wendel used his auxiliary function, thinking, to deal with the world in a critical manner. He was encouraged through counseling to view himself and others in less absolute terms. One way to accomplish this was to facilitate the development and use of his dominant intuition. Wendel needed to develop his perception (N) so that his judgments (T) were more balanced instead of prematurely formed. He was challenged to look for patterns, motivations, and needs within himself and others. Viewing the world and himself with intuition was new and exciting and seemed to free up some energy to deal with school. One of the factors in his lack of motivation was his harsh internal critic which never offered encouragement. Wendel was helped to understand these internal dynamics and to work on being less critical. He could rechannel his T into more productive activity such as analyzing information and ideas.

Another aspect of his unmotivated attitude was the lack of a career goal. Several career areas were suggested, related to his interests, abilities, and type. Some of these were: nutritional research, environmental studies/engineering, urban planning, natural resources management, forestry, biological/physical fitness research. Wendel's investigative INT was challenged to learn more about these career areas through reading, interviewing professionals in the field, a summer job, and possibly by volunteering in one of these fields. He planned to return in Fall for follow-up counseling. Wendel did return in Fall, still feeling frustrated with himself, the people around him, and the college in general.

He wanted to retake the MBTI and take the Strong Interest Inventory (SCII). He also wanted to discuss transferring to a larger school with more cf a vocational emphasis. Retesting confirmed INTJ preferences. The SCII was not helpful because he marked so many responses "dislike" that results on all scales were "average" or "low." Interests previously explored in our counseling sessions led him to choose forestry management as a tentative major. His MBTI preferences could find expression and satisfaction in that field. Wendel planned to transfer to a large state university offering this major but first wanted to spend some time traveling, camping, and working before returning to school.

Before Wendel left at the end of the term, we spent several more sessions working through his frustrations and continued self-criticism. Gestalt approaches were helpful in such areas as getting his discouraged self to confront his critical "top-dog" self through an experimental dialogue.

Several years later Wendel visited me and brought me up to date on what he had been doing. He had had several odd jobs to make money between outdoor expeditions. He was fiercely insistent on financial independence from his parents and lived a frugal, spartan lifestyle to achieve this independence. He had tried the state university but felt that the programs in forestry and environmental studies were "compromised" and not consistent with his ideals for the environment. His new goal was to look "outside the system" (outside conventional academic structures).

He was interested in utopian societies and self-supporting communities that existed in harmony with the land. As Wendel talked, he conveyed strong conviction and determination to research these utopian societies and help form one himself if he couldn't locate one already established. He had come to realize that his family and most others could not understand his vision and had accepted this. Although this visit was not a counseling session, I did remind him about type theory—that he might need to temper his inner visions with outer reality, talk over his ideas and perceptions with respected individuals, and be realistic in what he expected from himself, others, and the environment.

Wendel was more comfortable with himself and was no longer as restless and frustrated as in his student days. He had a sense of direction and an awareness of the motivators, values, and preferences which shaped his choices. Wendel stated that learning about the MBTI had been a significant event in his growth. The insight about himself and validation of that self had much impact. He acknowledged the possibility that he might not succeed on this new path, but by following the path he would learn a great deal about himself and the world. He felt compelled to proceed in this individualistic, non-traditional way. Wendel speculated that perhaps someday he would return to academics to teach or research utopian societies and related issues.

In summary, the MBTI was quite helpful to Wendel in affirming his strengths, his uniqueness, and his need to do things differently from many fellow students. He was able to view his preferences with some humor and not take himself as seriously. Although he had a strong need to live by severe, ascetic standards and principles, he had discovered that if he carried this style "too far" (his words), he just frustrated and depressed himself. Instead, he channeled his introverted intuition into investigative efforts and new possibilities and as an NT "visionary" conceptualized and evaluated systems (communities, institutions). Finally, his J preference led him to plan, structure, and persist.

INTROVERTED THINKING
with Intuition

INTP

Lorraine—INTP

The Need for Personal Space

When Lorraine arrived in my office immediately following referral by her academic advisor, she was in overload. Lorraine felt as if she would "burst" but didn't understand the origins of this feeling. She was very self-conscious about being in my office and about self-disclosing to someone she vaguely knew. Lorraine was a very private person who believed in solving problems deliberately and thoroughly by herself.

Lorraine was a bright student who was not doing her work and was so far behind that she was now paralyzed about catching up. She shed tears of frustration and expressed anger with "the system." The system of awarding financial aid was unfair in her eyes, penalizing her hard-working parents and expecting them to make heavy sacrifices. She felt guilty about being in school when her parents were struggling financially. She worried about her parents, their growing old, and her alienation from them. She was probably in the grip of her inferior feeling, causing her to exaggerate the emotional aspects of her relationship with her parents. Frequently INTPs, with dominant T and inferior F, present themselves in counseling when their inferior swamps their usually logical way of coping; they then feel so overwhelmed that they may seek counseling.

Concerns about her family were explored. She expressed remorse that she had treated them so indifferently in high school and now realized how estranged she was from them. Lorraine thought she might transfer to a college closer to home so she could build a new relationship with her parents. We also explored the possibility of her doing this relationship building over summer vacation. Part of this session focused on how she could develop better communications with her parents. Her natural style was to be brief and assume people knew what she meant or felt, especially characteristic of INTs. We worked on improving her skills to be more self-disclosing and verbally responsive. We rehearsed anticipated situations with her parents.

Through counseling, Lorraine also became aware that she was grieving over the loss of her personal space. Before coming to college, she had her own room and now had a roommate. Previously she had a car in which she could also "escape" when she needed privacy. Now she saw herself as "trapped" on campus without a car. She had come to resent people around her and felt alienated. Applying information about her MBTI preferences to her current concerns proved very helpful. Earlier in the year, we had reviewed her MBTI results, as part of the freshman testing program, and now revisited those results. As an INTP (particularly I), she needed time for herself every day and a place to be alone. We brainstormed private places she could go and how she could carve out quiet time from her schedule. Lorraine needed to give herself permission to take this time; she felt guilty about not spending that time studying (when her parents were sacrificing financially). She decided to drop one course to reduce the pressure and free-up more time. We also discussed her need to become more aware of feelings as they developed, instead of waiting until these feelings reached eruptive proportions. The quiet time was suggested as a good time to "go inside" and notice how she was feeling about herself and others. This suggestion was presented in a logical, matter-of-fact way with a systems/efficiency rationale that appealed to her thinking preference.

To create order in her world, Lorraine needed to introvert, since her dominant function was introverted thinking judgment. Just making time to introvert and to use her T for evaluating her activities and current situation could help Lorraine stabilize. She could learn to use her thinking judgment more effectively to prioritize and manage her time better. She also became aware that feeling was her least preferred function. Her difficulties in reading others' reactions and communicating about interpersonal nuances related to her undeveloped feeling function. By observing behavior of feeling types, she could increase her awareness of F so she could begin to recognize and develop it in herself.

She was encouraged to return for additional counseling to help her keep on track with her school work. I shared with her that many students with P preference, especially IPs can fall into a procrastination pattern because of their preference for doing things at the last minute and not structuring their time. Through counseling these students learn techniques to reduce procrastination. In my college practice, INTPs seem to have the most difficulty of all the 16 types (followed by the INFPs) with procrastination on written papers. Many of them have described their process as: needing to think or "stew" on ideas internally for a long time; feeling as if they never have enough information to get started; being perfectionistic about the first sentences written down and every written word; and subsequently becoming more and more overwhelmed by the task as time runs out.

Lorraine came for only two sessions. Her emotional crisis had passed. It had been difficult for her to open up to another, but her high level of stress had propelled her to do so. Now that the anxiety was reduced, she did not wish to continue the counseling process. She had a high need to operate independently but knew I was there as a resource. The MBTI validated her need for personal space and also her strengths as an individual (e.g. her creativity, curiosity, patience, and interest in theory). She was more motivated to do her academic work, having replenished her emotional/spiritual self with some private time. Energy previously tied up in feeling guilty about her parents was now redirected towards schoolwork. She was eager to spend time with her family and practice communications skills. At the end of the academic year, she transferred to a college closer to home. The counseling process had acknowledged Lorraine's individualistic style and fierce need for independence, while supporting her and offering her coping tools.

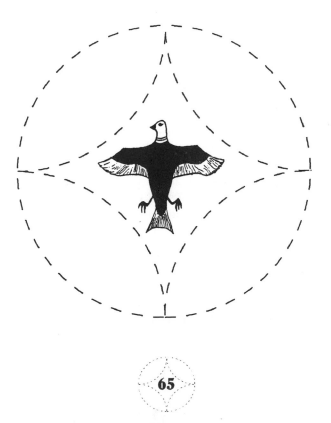

EXTRAVERTED INTUITION
with Thinking
ENTP

N
T
F
s

Billie—ENTP

The Unfocused Entrepreneur

Like Lorraine, Billie sought counseling during emotional overload. Billie self-referred following an extremely emotional confrontation with her mother over her two failed courses and generally poor academic performance. Billie was the oldest child of her widowed mother. She felt a great deal of pressure to succeed because of her place in the family and came to college with high expectations for success. Her excellent high school grades supported this expectation.

Billie appeared agitated, and her thought process was very scattered. She spoke rapidly and without focus. Using a Gestalt approach, she was directed to slow down and pay attention to body sensations and internal emotional impressions. She was asked to report in detail on everything she was experiencing in the "here and now." This task helped to ground and focus her. What emerged was an awareness of feeling like two people—a "superficial" self and a "true" self. Her superficial self was easily influenced by peers and was non-assertive. She lacked self-control, partied heavily, and was sexually active with many partners. Her "true" self was vulnerable and afraid of failing. This self wanted more self-control, assertive responsibility-taking, and academic and career direction.

Viewing her present college lifestyle, she expressed a desire to "turn over a new leaf," to work toward the goals of understanding herself and developing more self-control. The mutually set counseling goals were to:

∝ join an assertiveness training group
∝ work with the learning center to develop time management and study skills

∝ learn about aspects of herself through the MBTI
∝ set realistic goals for herself, including career/academic goals
∝ work on improving communications with her mother

Billie proved to be a poor candidate for the assertiveness group. Her energy level was almost hyperactive and her attention span so short that she could not contribute appropriately. The other group members were distracted by her. After one session she withdrew from the group and worked with me individually on assertiveness skills.

Billie began missing her individual appointments after a few sessions. She had difficulty staying focused in sessions and avoided deeper self-exploration by telling disconnected stories. When gently confronted with her avoidance behavior, she denied the behavior and stated she felt as if she were back in control and "everything was going right." At this time she admitted to heavy partying, involving use of alcohol and drugs, but was evasive about specific use. It was difficult to assess the degree of her use of alcohol and drugs. She appeared to be flitting from one campus activity to the next, in "butterfly" fashion. This butterfly behavior is a frequent characteristic of EPs who have not developed their judgment function. Billie did not use her thinking to evaluate appropriateness of behavior, consequences, or to prioritize activities. For example, she did not evaluate the consequence of her alcohol use in relation to her grades. She also seemed reluctant to work on developing her thinking through further counseling.

She was, however, interested in preliminary career exploration. The MBTI preferences were discussed in terms of her strengths with application to career areas. Her interests, energy, and type led to considering careers with outdoor and adventure components.

She was particularly interested in environmental studies and oceanography. With ability, these careers can be satisfying to the NTs because of their usual interest in abstract theories, sciences, technology, and systems. However, Billie expressed great impatience about the time one must spend in the classroom to prepare for these careers.

To channel her restless energy and interests, Billie decided to work part-time. She had a series of entrepreneurial sales jobs: creating art designs on surfboards, selling solar energy devices, etc. These jobs held more interest and were a higher priority to her than her studies. Billie followed a pattern similar to other male and female ENTP students I have counseled. The pattern involves academic problems in association with heavy drinking, partying, busying oneself with everything but academics, and stronger interest in the "real" world than in college. Often these students feel strongly pulled to go out and find adventure, make their own money, achieve independence. They are more likely than many of the other types to drop out of college temporarily or permanently to pursue these ends. These entrepreneurial ENTPs, so hungry for stimulation and excitement, often form their own businesses. I encourage those restless ENTPs who want a college degree, to work, volunteer, or have some noncollege activity while going to school. I also work with them to develop their thinking function, so that they can focus and direct their intuition and prioritize activities. Of course, as in Billie's case, clients may not be willing to continue counseling. In her case, substance abuse and the accompanying denial may have underlay her avoidance of counseling.

Billie was not ready for in-depth counseling, although by the end of that academic year, she had reduced the number of her extracurricular activities and was somewhat more organized about her studies. She still chose to approach living in a highly adventurous, non-conforming, and independent manner. Her approach to life was "to find out for myself." She withdrew at the end of that year and was unclear about whether she would work for a while or attend another college. Billie will probably seek counseling when the next crisis occurs.

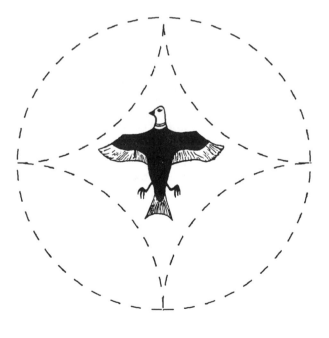

EXTRAVERTED SENSING
with Feeling

ESFP

Joy—ESFP

Spinning Her Wheels

Joy self-referred halfway through her freshman year because she was behind in all her school work and felt as if she were "going crazy." Like the other EPs in this casebook, she presented with agitation, dramatic gestures, and hysterical behavior.

Joy's relationships with her family and her boyfriend were her highest priorities. None of these relationships was satisfactory at the time she sought counseling. Consequently she could not concentrate on her studies. Her parents had divorced the previous year. She felt "in the middle" and had much unexpressed anger towards them. In the session she became aware of experiencing this anger as tension and shaking in her upper body. A Gestalt activity helped her to express this anger using her arms, pillows, and verbalizations. Joy's boyfriend had been the stabilizing force in her life during the past few years but was now more than 1000 miles away at another college. She felt a real loss of his support and felt the relationship was strained by the distance. Her way of coping was "spinning her wheels": sitting staring at her books and worrying about these relationships, or avoiding work altogether by socializing with other friends. Joy also distracted herself by getting involved in friends' personal problems.

As an ESFP, Joy sought high stimulation and action through the sensing channel, her dominant function. She needed to learn to introvert to access and to understand her feeling judgments. Introverting in this way could cause a shift from vague awareness of a "block" of feelings to awareness of the discreet feelings within. Pounding and squeezing pillows to focus her attention through action, followed by quiet assessment of what was happening inside, were helpful to her.

As she began to understand her feeling judgment as well as her emo-

tions and their origins, she became clearer about actions she could choose to take. She learned to use feeling judgment to sort out the events in her life and decide on actions based on her own needs and values. For example, her status-conscious parents pressured her to choose a career with prestige, such as law. Joy, on the other hand, was not interested in a lengthy education. She was interested in working with children. Yet, she had not asserted this with her parents; she had complied with their academic plans for her while resenting them. She had tried "not to rock the boat" while her parents were in marital conflict. Consequently Joy rebelled periodically by not studying or by acting out through petty conflict with her parents. Joy's counseling goals were to learn to be more assertive with her parents, to avoid "being in the middle" with them, to tell them about her interests in working with children, and to make career plans consistent with her needs.

In the second session, another counseling goal was mutually established: to help her achieve some personal balance by learning to use her thinking function. For example, her thinking function was engaged to analyze the chain of events and behaviors which precipitated a conflict with her parents. We examined links in the chain that could be broken to interrupt the fight sequence, such as: What were the cues that "hooked" her into fighting?; How could she respond differently? Joy responded well to this approach and to other thinking interventions such as applying Ellis' Rational Emotive Therapy to understand how her negative thinking influenced her emotional responses. She was ready to find a "more adult" way to respond to highly charged situations. Working with her thinking seemed to have a calming or balancing effect on Joy.

The MBTI was utilized to help her understand her present coping style and also to explore possible career directions. Although I had incorporated my knowledge of Joy's type into my counseling approach with her, MBTI concepts were not introduced explicitly until several sessions were devoted to her affective state. An earlier interpretation of her results would have been premature because of her emotional state and confusion. Her interests in children, coaching athletics, and working with recreational groups were supported. I have found that young ESFPs often are heavily involved in team sports in high school and even in the lower grades. They are group-oriented and love playful activity. They also tend to like and do well in coaching because of sensitivity to others' responses and their ability to generate enthusiasm. These characteristics, of course, can apply in child development careers as well. Joy's flexibility (P) and attention to practicalities (S) were also cited as useful in these careers. She felt more positively about herself, and decided to major in elementary education or early child development. She realized she would have to assert these plans with her parents to achieve her goals but also realized her former way of dealing with them was nonproductive and destructive. Joy made the decision to transfer to a school with her chosen academic major which was closer to her boyfriend.

Before she left, we did additional work on developing awareness of discreet feelings (as opposed to hysterical responses) and ways of expressing these feelings. She was encouraged to have an outlet through daily physical activity. Joy, like many ESPs, relied heavily on external factors, such as a boyfriend or peers, to shape her life. She regularly found herself reacting to these external factors with little reliance on an internal system of self-control. We explored ways she could develop an internal guidance system, using her evaluative or judging function. The judgment function could help her with time management and setting priorities based on her own needs, not just those of her friends.

Joy was motivated to work in counseling because her relationships were very important. It was also easy to develop rapport with her. She was able to succeed academically once she achieved a level of self-understanding. She ended counseling when she transferred. Joy left with a better sense of self, more confidence in her ability to interact with her parents as an adult, and anticipation of a personally meaningful career direction.

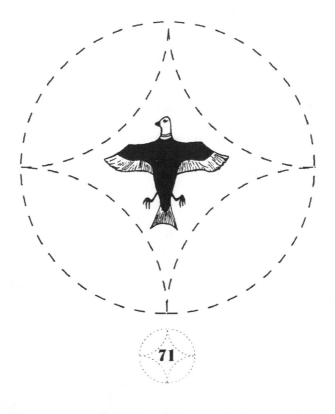

INTROVERTED THINKING
with Sensing

ISTP

T
S
N
F

James—ISTP

Freshman Panic

"Feeling is the least manageable process for an ISTP. If too suppressed, it can build up pressure and explode in most inappropriate ways." James' reactions during the first week of college are accurately described by this quote from CAPT's interpretive printout. He was referred to me by campus police following an outburst of potentially suicidal behavior. James had too much to drink, became morose and confused, felt alienated, panicked, and expressed thoughts of ending his life.

At first James was quite embarrassed by the referral for counseling and by all the attention he had attracted. He was encouraged to talk about his feelings, concerns, and tensions which had led to his acting out. James' predominant emotion was one of alienation, saying that the people at college were not "real," and therefore he couldn't relate to them. He missed his girlfriend back home; she had been a source of security and support. James' parents were both high achievers who expected great things from their son. James was not sure that college was for him. In fact, he had made a feeble suicidal gesture while going through the college application process the year before. It appeared that not only was he experiencing the loss of his previous support system but he also was feeling pressured by expectations to succeed academically and socially. In an intensive two hour session, he ventilated these thoughts and feelings. Although reluctant to do so at first, his anxiety propelled him to self-disclose. Talking appeared to bring relief. He expressed appreciation for the "meaningful contact" with me, his first "real" contact at college, according to him. The experience of disclosing feelings was new to James, and he was helped to see the value of expression using his preferred "language" of rationality and cause-effect (T). By attending to feelings as they occurred, James could avoid the build up which led to explosive crises and caught him off balance.

Frequently ITPs, in whom feeling is the least preferred function, are startled or even frightened by sudden bursts of emotion which seem to come from "nowhere." Their usual lack of orientation toward processing feelings and sorting out interpersonal reactions results in bewilderment about their emotions. They often do not have a vocabulary or framework to begin sorting and expressing these reactions. Dominant thinking is appropriately applied to data, ideas, and tasks. However, as in cases such as James, thinking is not very effective in sorting out intense personal and interpersonal reactions. Thus, when his usual thinking approach failed to control his strong reactions, panic resulted. A vicious cycle can emerge: strong emotional response, attempt to handle it through analytical, cause-effect thinking, continued strong emotion, and further panic at lack of control. The individual feels overwhelmed. Under these circumstances, ITPs may actually come under "the grip of the inferior" feeling function, which is very primitive. As in James' case, they exhibit childish emotional behavior and are concerned that they "don't belong," "that nobody likes them."

Clients in the grip of inferior feeling can be helped, first, by supporting expression of feelings in a safe, controlled environment. Next, counselors can appeal to the auxiliary sensing to get the client out of inferior feeling. It seems too enormous a shift to go from inferior feeling to dominant thinking. Appealing to his sensing, James was asked to look at the specifics in his current situation. By describing concretely what was happening in his life and looking at the practical implications, he was able to move out of the uncomfortable inferior onto more solid ground (sensing). Then the next step of moving James to his strength, thinking, became easier. James was led through a thinking analysis of how specific conditions led to certain emotional reactions (cause and effect). Emotions can be demystified so that they are less intimidating to dominant thinking clients.

After James' affect shifted from an explosive to a stabilized state, we focused on the process of adjustment to college, particularly the social aspects. How did he go about making contact with his peers? We discussed concrete behaviors that he could try; this concrete approach appealed to his sensing. He admitted to "posing" and "playing games" and was challenged to be more real. The importance of self-disclosure and trust in developing friendships was stressed. I suggested he also avoid drinking until he felt more comfortable on campus, since his drinking could precipitate another outburst or panic. I determined that James was not suicidal. He agreed to contact me immediately if he entertained further suicidal thoughts.

Finally, James was encouraged to continue counseling to practice attending to his feelings and to assist adjustment to college. James was reluctant to continue counseling, since he perceived his problem as immediate and transitory. I expressed respect for his decision but left the door open for further sessions and suggested he at least consider me a "safety valve" for expressing feelings. He said he felt relieved to know he was not alone. Like many other ISPs I have worked with, James' tendency was to seek brief counseling for a crisis only. We had not discussed his MBTI results in this single crisis intervention session but I encouraged him to return when he was ready to explore the MBTI in relation to academic work and career possibilities. Later in the year, James returned for consultation. He brought a friend with him. Both were seeking advice on how to help a mutual friend with a serious drinking problem. He also referred several other friends for counseling during the year. He appeared to view me as a resource and support. Yet he did not feel a need for growth or insight counseling. James said he now had a close network of friends, was handling the academic work successfully, and was pleased with his adjustment to college. Seeing him on campus, he appeared cheerful and socially involved.

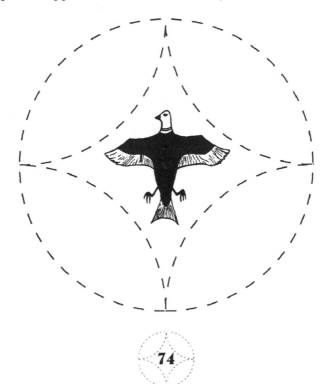

EXTRAVERTED SENSING WITH THINKING

ESTP

Dave—ESTP

Reluctant Student

Like James, Dave was referred for potentially suicidal behavior during a heavy drinking episode. He was embarrassed to have made "such a display" of his feelings and said he didn't feel as if he "fit in" at the college.

His family was far away, and he was having trouble initiating new friendships. In addition, Dave had recently received his first grades; two unsatisfactories at mid-term of his first semester. He was discouraged but not suicidal. He had no organized approach for studying. The several ensuing counseling sessions focused on social and academic adjustment.

One session was devoted to interpretation of his MBTI results. During discussion of ESTPs' preferences for immediacy, action, and direct sensing experience, Dave admitted that he really did not want to be in college. His parents had pressured him with their expectations that he should become a "professional." Dave wanted to become a flight attendant instead of going to college. He was resentful and angry, especially towards his father, but had never expressed his feelings and desires to his parents. Instead his solution was to "go around" his parents, satisfying their basic demands so that he could reap material benefits from them. He was reluctant to "rock the boat" because financial support might be cut off. Material comforts were a high priority to him.

We rehearsed how he might assertively communicate to his parents his feelings about college and his career without causing intense conflict. Since Dave saw no virtue in communicating feelings, practical reasons were offered, appealing to his sensing preference; e.g. unexpressed resentment could get in the way of his functioning at school and elsewhere. Furthermore, his parents were not mind readers; he needed to let them know his desires. The MBTI indicated preferences which might be attracted to careers within the airlines, such as pilot, operations officer, or possibly flight attendant. More Fs than Ts would be expected in this latter occupation because of required sensitivity to passenger needs. SFs are more likely to seek service jobs. ESTPs usually are "trouble shooters," often good at sizing up the needs of the moment and operating quickly with common sense and objectivity. These strengths are helpful in unpredictable and changeable circumstances, such as in the travel industries. Of course, it was pointed out to Dave that other career areas could also utilize these strengths.

Often ESTPs have difficulty feeling motivated to do academic work unless they have well-formulated, practical goals. Distribution requirements, such as an introductory philosophy course, may seem meaningless and irrelevant to them. Like many other Ps, they often are not organized in study habits. Therefore, in addition to exploring the meaning of college for Dave, I encouraged him to attend the Learning Skills Center to develop better study skills. I stressed that he would enjoy college more with these acquired skills (and enjoyment is a strong motivator for most ESTPs).

Dave's concerns about his social adjustment were first met with supportive statements about the typical adjustment patterns of most freshmen. Some examples of others' similar experiences and a simple explanation of the usual struggles that go with this stage of transition to college helped to normalize his experience. I was fairly direct and more informative than I might be working with an intuitive client, because Dave's dominant was sensing. Also his least developed function was N, and the pattern of his transition to college was not apparent to him. We examined available opportunities for developing new friends and getting involved. Since he had been socially successful in high school, he did not seem to need social skill building but rather just encouragement and reassurance.

After a few sessions, Dave had become more involved on campus and felt good about his new college friends. He was unwilling to be open with his parents as yet. He had decided "to stick it out" for his freshman year and then try to get a job with the airlines. He was encouraged to return for additional counseling as needed and to let me know how he was doing. Dave remained in college and consulted with me periodically when he perceived himself as needing guidance in a specific situation. He was active in a fraternity, maintained a C average, but had not yet finalized his career plans.

Dave had been very self-conscious in initial counseling sessions, expressing concern that he had acted foolishly. Although he was motivated to resolve his anxieties about being in college, he did not wish to probe deeply into his own intrapsychic functioning.

Like many ESs, he wanted to take quick action. The MBTI was a useful tool for many reasons but especially for discriminating whether Dave's reaction to college was purely parental rebellion or whether in part it was a reflection of his own nature.

INTROVERTED FEELING
with Sensing

ISFP

Carmen—ISFP

Somatic Complaints

Like many other ISFPs and the ISTP and ESTP cases presented earlier, Carmen was referred in crisis and terminated counseling as soon as the crisis was resolved. Carmen was referred to me by the college physician who had treated her for acute gastric distress.

Carmen was emotionally overloaded. Her boyfriend had just been arrested for drug dealing and placed in an involuntary treatment program. Her parents had just separated, each taking one of the children and "splitting the family in half." Carmen felt as if she had lost her family, her home, her boyfriend and feared also losing her student status. She could not concentrate on studies and was already on academic probation.

I encouraged her to follow the physician's treatment plan for her gastric symptoms and to discuss her academic status with her faculty advisor. Then we focused on identification and expression of specific feelings related to her concerns. She saw the connection between her gastric symptoms and her emotional distress over her relationships. Carmen expressed relief at being heard and understood by someone; she had felt so alone in her crisis. Carmen needed a great deal of support and some stability in her currently chaotic life. Doing well academically so she could stay in school was one way to achieve some stability. Carmen tended to focus on emotional issues over which she had no control. This focus increased her anxiety which she held in, leading to gastric symptoms. In my caseload, many dominant introverted feeling types somatize to their digestive systems under stress. Once she had ventilated feelings, she was ready for a problem solving mode. Utilizing her preference for sensing, I asked her to focus on issues she could do something about, practically speaking. The drug treatment program would not allow her to contact her boyfriend; she thus felt helpless in regard to him. Carmen could dispel some of this helplessness by contacting the program director and learning specifics about her treatment. This small step gave her a sense of being more in control. She also needed to talk to both of her parents about not being put in the middle or not having to chose sides. We role played several conversations with her parents in which she expressed her emotional need for both of them. I modeled specific communication skills to use with her parents. She was encouraged to allow herself to grieve over the loss of her home. The process of grieving was explained as a necessary one for her to get on with her own life.

The MBTI suggested ways I could utilize Carmen's strengths to cope with her crisis. Affirming and supporting her dominant feeling calmed and steadied Carmen. Her auxiliary sensing seemed well-developed for dealing with the external world. With encouragement she was able to use her sensing to find practical solutions and take each moment as it came.

In the next session we further explored her academic situation and how the MBTI could be applied. We discussed ISFPs' usual learning style and study habits. Like many other ISFPs she was somewhat of a "free spirit" about studying. She was shown some methods for becoming more organized. She was referred to a study techniques workshop and to tutors. We explored the potential "traps" for her type that could prevent her from sticking to her study plan. For example, anxieties or bottled up feelings needed to be expressed or she would not be able to concentrate on schoolwork. Her preference for P could cause her to rebel against too rigid a schedule, especially if she didn't build in some social, fun rewards for completing parts of her schedule. She was motivated to improve her studying because completing school would please her family and give her status. Intellectual achievement in itself was not a motivator. Carmen worked with her advisor and tutors to improve her grades.

Her advisor and a college administrator served as parental figures who could regularly check on her progress. These professionals were influences on her to become more responsible and organized. Carmen was encouraged to touch base with me periodically for support and continuity. She reported better communications with her parents, understanding and acceptance of her boyfriend's situation, improvement of her physical condition, and generally feeling calmer. Carmen worked hard enough to remove herself from academic probation and graduated with the rest of her class.

EXTRAVERTED FEELING
with Sensing

ESFJ

Richard—ESFJ

The Need to Please

Richard, age 19, self-referred with many questions about interpersonal relationships. He was unhappy with his friendships and felt he was being used by his friends. He said he was always giving to others materially and emotionally. Yet he felt his friends rarely reciprocated. Richard assumed that friends should know that he needed the same kinds of attention and caring he gave to them. He was criticized by his parents for spending too much money on his friends. His pattern was to interact with effusive warmth, often offering gifts or favors, and then to feel hurt and resentful when he was not appreciated.

We briefly discussed the relevance of his MBTI results to his interactions. Since his dominant function was extraverted feeling, harmony and approval were crucial. Richard had difficulty saying no to friends' requests, as many dominant feeling types do. Also as an SJ, especially SFJ, he needed expressions of appreciation from friends for "the little things" he did for them. From our discussion, Richard learned that the other 15 MBTI types had different values and ways of interacting. Therefore, Richard could not assume that his friends could "know" what he needed from them, or that they even valued the same things. This insight was particularly helpful to him, although he regretted having to adjust his way of thinking (others "should feel the same way").

Richard was the youngest of four and had always played the harmonizer and pleaser role in his family. His mother could always count on him to run errands when the other children refused. His parents disapproved of his pursuing an academic major in the performing arts. Since he was concerned about pleasing his parents, his interest in the performing arts created a conflict.

Much of our work centered on challenging his irrational belief that he "must please everybody." Albert Ellis' Rational Emotive Therapy was used to help him examine his thoughts and beliefs about people and himself. Rational Therapy stimulates use of the thinking function in systematically analyzing and objectively evaluating beliefs/self-talk. This therapeutic approach has been particularly helpful with feeling types in helping them develop some use of their thinking function. This approach must be introduced gently to Fs, however, after rapport is established. If cognitive therapy is introduced too early in the counseling process, feeling clients may reject the therapist and this therapeutic approach as "cold, insensitive and irrelevant" to them.

Assertiveness training helped Richard decrease the number of situations where he felt used. Specific techniques were taught and practiced on how to say no and how to ask for what he needed from his friends. Richard responded very positively to this training, returning to report new successes in relating to his friends. He needed encouragement and support for trying these new behaviors, because he had such strong self-talk that he must be "nice to everyone." The structured assertiveness techniques appealed to his SJ preferences for structure and practical direction. Assertiveness training also stimulates the thinking function, since the client must answer the question, "What are my personal rights here?" and analyze behavioral choices and consequences.

Another practical intervention was to work on his breathing to interrupt anxiety reactions. When conflict emerged in a relationship, he began to breathe shallowly, talk faster, get more and more flustered and become unable to communicate assertively. This breathing response to anxiety could be observed during counseling. His experience with voice lessons had taught him a method of deep breathing which he could employ to interrupt his anxiety cycle. He was instructed to monitor his rate of speech, breathing, and feelings and to use breathing to calm himself. Because this suggestion took advantage of his natural preference for sensing, he was enthusiastic and successful with this technique.

Richard responded well to counseling because of his motivation to change his relationships and because of the rapport developed in the counseling sessions. The MBTI suggested interventions that would assist in his type development and was helpful to Richard in understanding individual differences. Counseling sessions spanned most of one school year on an irregular schedule. After termination of the counseling relationship, Richard came by periodically to chat briefly and let me know that things were going well for him. He continued with his theater major and established a more satisfying, adult relationship with his family.

EXTRAVERTED THINKING
with Sensing

ESTJ

T
S
N
F

Roger—ESTJ

Discomfort with the Unknown

Although I had known Roger as a student leader for four years and consulted with him about student organizations, he had never sought counseling until early Spring of his senior year. Roger had always been extremely decisive and organized but suddenly found himself in an indecisive, bewildered condition. He expressed anxiety about his future and requested the MBTI to help him in planning and deciding about the future.

Roger scored very clear preferences for ESTJ. He had questions about whether to go to law school or get an MBA. Should he go right on to graduate school or work for a while? Should he choose a geographical area close to his family, or just take the best opportunity? Although most seniors experience anxiety over these kinds of decisions, Roger's anxiety was intensified because of his MBTI preferences for resolving things quickly and concretely. He was impatient with himself and concerned about making "the right" decision.

Basic counselor attending and values clarification helped him clarify his present feelings and attitudes. Although Roger was tired of school, he liked the security of a (graduate) school structure and the familiarity of the student role. Looking at the strengths of his type and his past work/life experiences, we identified the kinds of work he might find satisfying: day-to-day business management in a large, well-organized firm with a great deal of people contact. We structured a job search plan, which appealed to his ESTJ approach of organization and practicality. The issue of security in relation to family was also explored. He was able to express his fear of making the major transition from school to the adult world. Roger was encouraged to weigh his need for family support versus a good job distant from family. He was cautioned not to resolve things too quickly just to have a decision made. Too quick closure or foreclosure can be a problem in the decision making of ESTJs, especially young ones. He gave himself permission to postpone temporarily a decision about job location so he could remain open to possibilities and to awareness of his emotional needs. In type terms Roger used his dominant thinking to weigh his options using a cost-benefit approach, identifying consequences for each option. He was encouraged to take enough time to use his sensing as well to gather sufficient information on his options. Roger was also reminded to factor in his personal needs (feeling) and given logical reasons for doing so. Like many dominant thinking types, he generally pushed aside his emotional responses and needs.

Later in Spring, Roger returned in a panic about what he termed "acute senioritis." He had been skipping classes and "even a test," which was totally uncharacteristic of him (and of ESTJs in general). He didn't like these behaviors, and yet he couldn't get motivated. His anxieties about transition to the adult world were sabotaging his attempts to study. Continued exploration of these feelings allowed him to better focus on his studies. Unfortunately, his course load was so light that he could put off working, but then he couldn't get back into the work mode. In other words, he had lost his familiar work/study structure and felt generally lost. Roger also experienced guilt because his former conscientious, achieving ways had been replaced by "laziness."

My intervention was somewhat paradoxical. It gave Roger the opportunity to socialize and play more, which he wanted during his last months at school. Yet the intervention also gave him a structure in which to function. After examining his course load, I encouraged him to "allow" himself to study ONLY two days a week, no more. (It was realistic for him to complete his work in that time period.) On these two work days he was to work very hard and not play. The rest of the week he should not work but should socialize, job search, etc. Roger grinned broadly at this plan. He had never before been told *not* to study.

Upon follow-up one week later and again after three weeks, Roger was enjoying his schoolwork and his social life. He grinned and said, "It's working!" He continued to do well academically. We worked through a step-by-step decision making process for his post graduation plans. The MBTI in some ways gave him permission to fear the unknown and to desire security, since these are important issues for many STJs. At the same time, his strengths for the job market were validated by the MBTI, increasing his confidence to find a job and to pursue graduate school when he was ready. Following graduation he accepted a promising position in a management training program, close enough to his parents for weekend visits. Although ESTJ students are not as likely to seek ongoing, growth-oriented counseling, students like Roger are eager for short term, structured interventions that meet their immediate needs.

EXTRAVERTED THINKING
with Intuition

ENTJ

T
N
S
𝓕

Mara—ENTJ

Developing Tact and Patience

Mara was referred by the college physician the second week of school because of nervousness and difficulty sleeping. Mara appeared to be struggling to hold herself together and was extremely tense. Home was far away. She was feeling the loss not only of her family but also of her psychiatrist with whom she had worked weekly for several years. The psychiatrist had been her "only emotional outlet"; she had not confided in family or peers. Suddenly she had no outlet and felt extremely tense. Talking gave her insight about the significance of this loss and brought an outburst of tears and subsequent relief. She had felt embarrassed to cry in front of her roommate and had invested a lot of energy in trying to cover up her anxiety. Mara also put pressure on herself to do well socially and academically in college.

Mara was encouraged to share feelings with her roommate. The rationale for expression of feelings was phrased in logical terms to appeal to her thinking. It was also apparent that she had difficulty in identifying emerging feelings and might not become aware of them until they reached eruptive proportions. Feeling was her least-preferred function. One of our counseling goals was to help her identify feelings sooner and learn to express them. Feelings, it was explained, had a physiological reality, "as real as facts," and must be dealt with.

Mara was encouraged to develop new friendships that could be a support and outlet for her. She had difficulty forming friendships, however, because she "came on too strong" and often treated others with impatience. If a conflict arose, she tended to state her opinion tactlessly and alienate her friend. We spent several sessions on assertive, as opposed to aggressive, ways of handling conflict and of communicating in general.

Besides having a social outlet, she was encouraged to get regular physical activity to help with sleeping. I also taught her a relaxation exercise to use during study times and at bedtime.

Several weeks later she was pleased to report she was sleeping better and had followed my suggestions. She was sharing more with her roommate and found her to be surprisingly receptive and supportive. She also was more aware of how she communicated with others.

Later in the year, Mara came hack to discuss academic majors in relation to her MBTI preferences for ENTJ. She expressed an interest in psychology and in marketing. Industrial psychology and marketing could be opportunities to channel ENTJ strengths: e.g., a natural desire to lead; an interest in creating, analyzing, and changing systems; a tendency towards long-range planning and structuring; impersonal objectivity; a desire for innovation and creativity; a liking for intellectual challenge and complexity. Mara was encouraged to sample courses in these areas and also plan some "real world" experiences in these areas, such as internships.

Mara saw me periodically whenever she became frustrated with her social situation. She tended to attach herself to a boyfriend and depend on this one individual for her intimacy needs. This was easier for her than establishing and maintaining several other friendships, especially with women. She did have many superficial friendships. When the boyfriend relationship was in trouble, she became anxious. After several boyfriends and several crises, I confronted her about this pattern. Mara began to work more deliberately towards a broader social base. She continued to battle with her impatience towards others and herself. Her NT desire for mastery, coupled with her EJ action/completion preferences contributed to this impatience. She was not naturally empathic and had to work to become more sensitive to others' responses. She was motivated to work at this because of her emotional needs and career ambitions. She saw that interpersonal skills would be important in her career. Mara made a reasonable adjustment during her first year in college. Mara did not contact me for further counseling. When seen later around campus, she seemed to be functioning well and graduated with a major in psychology.

EXTRAVERTED FEELING
with Intuition

ENFJ

Tom—ENFJ

Guilt and Self-Punishment

Tom was referred by his academic advisor because he seemed to be drifting in college, when by now, as a junior, he should have had more direction. Tom was interested in learning his MBTI results and how these might apply to several career considerations. First we discussed his interests in business, sales, law school or graduate school. Then we examined these interests in light of his preferences for ENFJ. His highly interactive style and interest in working with groups could be applied to many business settings. His extraverted energy and preferences for structure could apply to many of these career areas. Some cautions about law were discussed since he had a very clear preference for feeling. The majority of attorneys are thinking types. This fact was not presented as a deterrent to the selection of law as a career, but rather as an opportunity for him to examine his own motives and interests in law. Also, he was encouraged to learn more about this field in terms of day-to-day functioning.

Type should never be used to discourage someone from a career, nor to predict success. Where someone like Tom expresses interest in a career not typical for his type, the person's motivation, interests, and real knowledge of that career should be explored. An underrepresented type in a particular field might make a special contribution not made by the more frequent types. On the other hand, the underrepresented type might have false impressions and misinformation about the actual field, which need to be corrected for an appropriate career decision to be made.

I encouraged him to continue our sessions on career planning, since discussion of the MBTI was only a start. I sensed a reluctance on his part to continue counseling, and again his word "drifting" seemed to fit even in the counseling process.

I saw Tom a few months later when he was referred again, this time by the college physician after an episode of heavy drinking in which he seriously injured himself. Tom said he was relieved to be referred to me again and had been thinking of coming back to talk to me about personal issues. The drinking incident was a culmination of several others that year. This episode, however, had severely frightened him because of his "self-destructive tendencies." Tom felt as if he were out-of-control about his drinking, his impulsive behavior, and his study habits. His impulse at that moment was to run, to get away from the peer pressure to party, so he could "sort things out." I suggested he first get some food and rest and think about the questions he needed to ask himself. He was being encouraged to introvert and access his intuition, as well as to get some rest before making any decision. I asked him to return the next morning so we could explore the question of his leaving school or other options. I also took a drinking history and determined (assuming he was truthful) that he was not alcoholic. His alcohol use at this point seemed symptomatic of some underlying emotional problem.

The following morning Tom returned in much better physical condition with a clearer mind. We began to explore his lack of motivation at school, self-destructive impulses, and underlying depression. He was suffering a loss of self-esteem. In high school he had been the high achieving "good" student, whereas now he was behaving "irresponsibly." He judged himself harshly and did not like himself. He seemed to be in his inferior Thinking function, a primitive self-critic.

I discovered in the counseling process that his father had died a year ago that month, but that Tom's grieving had been attenuated.

At the time of his father's death, Tom had allowed himself a brief emotional outburst but then had "run away" from the family's grieving and returned to school. His feelings about his father, which he had shelved, were now reemerging on the anniversary of his death. His mother had been highly emotional during his father's illness and especially after his death. Tom felt overloaded by his mother's desire to lean on him as the only son. He needed to lean, too, but found no one to support him. So he had "escaped" to school. Yet he felt guilty and bad for "abandoning" his family.

Tom had another issue in regard to his father. He discovered in counseling that he harbored anger and resentment towards his father for never having been there for him when Tom was a child. His father had been in a business requiring a great deal of travel.

In order to finish grieving and relieve his depression, Tom needed to express these feelings toward his father. Tom was able to do this by imagining his father present in the counseling session and speaking to him.

I then asked Tom what he wished to do about his strained relationship with his mother. Tom realized that to feel better about himself he needed to "make things right" with his mother. We then roleplayed what he needed to say to his mother. He looked forward to the coming summer vacation when he could return home and repair this relationship.

Tom was given acceptance and respect for feelings towards his family. He was helped to express and clarify powerful emotions he had tried to suppress but which had affected his ability to function. He was guided towards understanding the grieving process and thus gained insight about his responses to his father's death. I challenged Tom to use his intuition and look at the pattern of his school behavior in light of these feelings we had uncovered. Tom's auxiliary function was fairly well-developed. With some encouragement to go inside (to introvert) and take the time to use his intuition, he arrived at some insights. He saw that his heavy drinking and related behaviors were a way to punish himself and confirm his "badness" in relation to his family. He expressed surprise at how these feelings, avoided for so long, had affected his behaviors and sense of self. He was now ready to forgive himself for running from his family. As an ENFJ, he had set very high expectations for himself about being a good son, but was now ready to see himself as more human than superhuman. He had done the best he could at the time. He felt back in control of himself and ready to give more to his family and to himself. Tom, now less stressed, was less often in the grip of his self-critical inferior thinking. We had no further counseling contact, although he knew the door was always open. Tom graduated the following year.

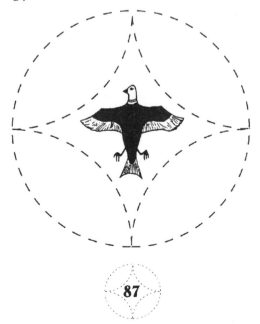

CHAPTER FIVE

Couples Counseling

uggestions for using the MBTI with individuals need to be sup-
plemented when applying the Indicator to couples work. For our
purposes couples may be heterosexual or homosexual, married
or living together, in a committed relationship. The MBTI is a valuable
tool widely used in premarital counseling and couples enrichment. The
MBTI is also useful in couples counseling which is problem focused.

There is much debate about which types choose each other as partners and whether there are some combinations that are better than others. Myers' (1980) data on 375 couples found "more similarity than
difference" (p.128). The most frequent similarity was on the SN dimension. The percentage of similarity for couples in her sample was:

Alike on all 4 dimensions	9%
Alike on 3	35%
Alike on 2	33%
Alike on 1	19%
Alike on none	4%

A recent study (Cohen, 1992) found support for the "completion
theory" of mate selection where mates seek to fulfill undeveloped qualities of the self. This study found differences in the mental functions
(S, N, T, F) more frequent than similarity within the sample of couples. Differences were not significant for E-I and J-P, however. Jung
used the term "compensatory mate selection" but stressed complementarity on the E-I dimension.

My own observations over the past twenty years are that young people are more likely to choose a partner who has different MBTI preferences, as in the old saying "opposites attract." One way of explaining
this pattern is to view such a partnership as having all the typological
"bases covered." An INFP and ISTJ may choose each other because they
admire each other's qualities, which they themselves don't possess.

Usually it is comforting having a partner who is "good at" the things the other is not so comfortable doing. There's a natural complementarity. Unconsciously the choice of a partner very different from oneself sets up the opportunity to develop the least preferred functions by observing good modeling of those functions in the partner. At first this choice is a way of *externally* acquiring functions absent from the conscious self or persona. As time passes, partners begin to practice the functions modeled by the other and begin to discover an *internal* source of these functions. Often it's helpful to point out this process to couples who are having difficulties because they are different. Couples often lose sight of why they chose each other and can be encouraged to reminisce about their courtship, choice, and the initial perceived value of partner differences.

Just as I have observed that young, and especially first time partnerships, are more likely to be different types, I've observed that more mature individuals, usually with several relationships behind them, are more likely to choose someone with more shared preferences. One explanation, consistent with that given for young partner choices, is that older individuals do not have as pressing a need for acquiring their least preferred functions in the other. With maturity they may have developed some use of their third and fourth functions and are therefore less drawn to finding these in a partner. One could also argue that those who have had several relationships with partners very different from themselves may deliberately seek someone more like themselves if they perceived the past relationships as too conflicted. In any case, type development issues tend to play out differently in partnerships formed later in life than in partnerships formed while young.

AFFIRMING THE LEGITIMACY OF EACH PARTNER

We've seen how the MBTI is a powerful tool for affirming an individual. Interpreting the MBTI to partners together has a great deal of affirmative power as well. Not only does each person feel affirmed, but this is witnessed by their partner. Witnessing the counselor, a third party, describing their partner's preferences, presents an important new perspective about their partner. A tone is set in counseling for the value and legitimacy of each partner. This is a crucial message that needs to be embedded in all couples work. Two people come together in relationship to form a "WE," yet they also remain separate "I's," each valuable and legitimate in his/her own right. This use of the MBTI is a subtle way for beginning to clarify ego boundaries, especially in situations where partners have lost sight of their own identities.

FINDING COMMONALITIES

Sometimes couples seeking counseling are so caught up in their differences that they have lost sight of common ground. There are many counseling interventions that can be used; type is one of them. One couple, an INTP and INFP, married for five years, were dissatisfied with their relationship. They complained that they had nothing to talk about because their interests were so different. He (INTP) liked theoretical history and tinkering with computers; she (INFP) liked the arts. These interests are typical for their Jungian types, but they were in a subtle power struggle for whose world view was "better" or "more legitimate"... the arts or technological systems. They were led through a series of explorations about their lifestyle, how they approached vacations, managed money, etc. in relation to their types. They were surprised to see from a new perspective that they *shared* many preferences for approaching life. Both used intuition in the outer world to see the possibilities. Both liked a very low-key flexible way of living. They reaffirmed these shared values and their INP similarities while acknowledging their differences in dominant (T vs. F). This new perspective did not resolve all their difficulties, of course, but did help build a positive foundation for further change.

Another couple who were very different, ESTJ and ENFP, found that their shared extraversion was a very important bridge. They both needed a high level of activity and engagement in the world around them, so they found *doing* things together was a way of building relationship. Through understanding type they could view with humor the realization that although they enjoyed a shared activity, they usually disagreed when communicating afterwards about what each had experienced. Their differences in ST and NF ways of processing experience were like two different languages. Instead of focusing on this difference, they learned to focus more on the real satisfaction in the shared activity. Finding commonalities provides a position of comfort and relative safety, then, to begin accepting differences.

UNDERSTANDING AND RESPECTING DIFFERENCES

Differences in preference can be a source of misunderstanding, conflict, and power struggle. These same differences can be a source of complementarity, fascination, and discovery. The counselor can be a catalyst for shifting the couple's perspective from the negative to the positive.

When couples present for counseling, they are often "dug in" about their differences, each defending his/her own position and accusing the other. By using the MBTI to identify preferences, differences are cast in a more objective and new light. Partners can see that many of their differences are related to natural preferences and not to deliberate efforts to be contrary or controlling.

Of course, not all differences and conflicts are type related. A new perspective on their differences diffuses some of the emotional charge and frees them up to consider other possible responses to each other.

Partners are much more likely to respect type differences once their own type has been affirmed. When individuals feel attacked and are defended, they are unable to recognize or affirm their partners. A first step is affirming the legitimacy of the other, no matter how different.

A next step can be for the counselor to explore with the couple how each makes certain contributions to the relationship because of his/her type. They can examine various areas of their lives such as: parenting, household management, leisure, vacations. The counselor may have to guide this discussion carefully so that the focus doesn't shift from what each *contributes* to disagreements about how to handle money, etc. Conflicts will need to be addressed later, but the purpose of this intervention is to appreciate and respect differences.

The ESTJ—ENFP couple mentioned earlier were able to identify and appreciate the following contributions each made related to vacations:

The ENFP contributed by:

∝ coming up with new and interesting possibilities
∝ providing enthusiasm for vacation options
∝ supporting and encouraging the ESTJ's planning efforts
∝ coming up with spontaneous modifications during the vacation and problem solving for unanticipated events

The ESTJ contributed by:

∝ researching the vacation possibilities and gathering facts
∝ making reservations
∝ forming an itinerary/plan
∝ checking that all necessary details were taken care of

Although this couple may have conflicts over some issues related to vacationing together, they can keep this in perspective with what they *appreciate* about each other as well. This strategy helps couples move from a "black and white," "all good vs. all bad" way of viewing their relationship to a "satisfying *and* frustrating" view.

REFRAMING CONFLICTS

The steps of affirming the legitimacy of each partner's type, understanding differences, and recognizing the contributions these differences can make to the relationship are useful precursors to reframing conflicts. The MBTI is *only one* intervention of many that couples therapists can use in helping couples handle conflict.

One couple reported that most of their fighting occurred in the first half hour after the husband came home from work. His preferences were INTJ and hers were ESFJ. The counselor suggested the couple look at their type preferences to see if there might be clues as to why conflict arose particularly in this situation. His work required him to extravert continually, meeting a variety of people in the course of the day, persuasively selling them on a product, and being the charming host. Her work was primarily in the home, including caring for a young child. She had little adult contact during the day, other than by phone, and was very eager to engage her husband in conversation as soon as he came through the door. She usually had compiled a list of specific, practical tasks or decisions she wanted his help with. It was natural to her type to want to talk about her list as soon as she greeted him. Their child was also eager for attention from daddy. As an Introvert he felt depleted from extraverting all day and needed some "decompression time" after work. Instead, when he came home to his perceived "sanctuary," he was greeted by demands to interact and to address household problems. He became instantly irritable, impatient, and withdrawn. Her response was to push harder for interaction, first with "What's wrong? Did I do something wrong? Talk to me." When he didn't fully respond, she shifted to frustration and anger and became more demanding and sometimes accusatory. "You never want to talk. You don't care about us" and so on. As the counselor and couple looked at these patterns in light of his preference for introversion and hers for extraversion with extraverted feeling dominant, they could reframe the problem. Each needed to compensate for their day and satisfy the needs of their types. The problem shifted from "Why doesn't he care?" and "She's a nag" to "How can we each get what we need and still respect the differing need of our partner?"

This couple brainstormed ways that he could have decompression time before interacting with his family. He could:

∝ take the long way home, using travel time to introvert and restore his energy.
∝ go from work directly to a workout location where he could do a solitary workout such as swimming laps or jogging.

93

∝ have half to one hour alone time once he got home to read, putter in the yard, jog.

The last option involved further negotiation. They could embrace warmly and then say, "See you in half an hour," with no further conversation. Or they could experiment with some variation of this.

She would need to say to herself that if she pushed him for more, she was not likely to get what she wanted anyway. She would get conflict instead. She needed assurance that once he had his alone time he would be truly available to her. He needed to understand how crucial this was to her. He might actually need a longer decompression time than the half hour, but he would need to find the additional time later in the evening or early the next morning. Through this intervention each was beginning to understand and respect the individuality of the other and learn productive problem solving for conflicts.

The example of this extravert-introvert conflict is one of the most frequent type-related conflicts, interaction vs. solitude. Sherman (1981) reported a study of couples in conflict and found that the greatest conflict occurred in couples where the man worked outside the home and was introverted and the woman worked inside the home and was extraverted. Today the stereotypical roles of woman as homemaker and man as breadwinner are much less frequent, but the issues of E-I differences are still valid with any couple. These differences become especially noteworthy when the partner's day does not accommodate the expression of the E or I preference (such as the INTJ having to extravert at work).

The same approach could be used to look at conflict in other situations and other type dimensions. Basically the therapist is teaching the couple a problem solving model involving type:

∝ When does conflict occur? What is the pattern?
∝ What is each feeling, thinking, needing?
∝ What are each's needs and approaches from a type perspective?
∝ Does looking at type explain some of the conflict and suggest a focus for problem solving?
∝ What can each live with (compromise)? What is each willing to try on a trial basis?
∝ What is the trial plan and when will they sit down together to evaluate how well it's working and whether modifications need to be made?

IMPROVING BASIC COMMUNICATIONS

When interpreting the MBTI to couples, counselors can describe communication styles, dimension by dimension, as a way of illustrating the preferences and bringing them to life. It is also important to get examples from the clients so the counselor is sure clients are understanding the concepts. Assuming that readers already understand the basic characteristics of each preference, the following list offers some additional observations of potential sources of miscommunication. These can be explored during initial interpretation or as problems are spotted during counseling sessions. These observations are *tendencies* and not absolutes for any specific individual. Individual variation exists within the types; many other factors influence behaviors.

EXTRAVERSION	INTROVERSION
Speaker's words are "in process" and not necessarily the final thought.	Speaker's words are the end product of thought.

[Opposites assume the other is using words the same way.]

Immediacy or quick response able.	Thoughtfulness and deliberation desireable.

[Opposites often have pacing difficulties.]

Need to say things out loud, to name feelings and thoughts in order to understand a situation.	Need to process internally and may not show this to partner.

[E's may perceive I's as being deliberately secretive; I's may not recognize E's need to talk it out.]

SENSING	INTUITION
Talks about specifics, here and now.	Talks in generalities, future oriented.
Sees things as they actually are on the surface.	Reads into things, speculates.
Takes things at face value.	Sees the symbolism of something or action.

[Miscommunication usually involves conflicting descriptions and interpretations of situations or experiences.]

Need to tell a story/experience from the very beginning sequentially and gets flustered by interruptions; will return to the place interrupted, insisting on telling in detail and sequence.	Skips around in telling an experience, leaving out details. Has a way of speaking associatively and often tangentially.

[These differences can lead to impatience and frustration about the way the opposite is telling an experience; the opposite may tune out.]

THINKING	FEELING
Talks about things and opinions but rarely about emotions.	Talks about emotions and people more than about things.

[Fs often believe Ts are deliberately withholding their emotional reactions when in actuality Ts are using a different language to discuss their reactions. Ts can become frustrated with the lack of precision and "over-expressiveness" of Fs.]

Evaluates situations logically, in terms of cause-effect, "the bottom line is . . ."	Evaluates the "Gestalt" or whole quality of situation based on nuances of interaction and personal values.

[Many arguments center on these opposite ways of deciding and evaluating. Word choices differ for Ts and for Fs. Fs can interpret T communication as impersonal and uncaring. Ts can interpret Fs as vague, too subjective, and bewildering.]

JUDGING	PERCEIVING
Focuses on the outcome of discussion or problem.	Focuses on the process of *how* couple interacts.
May rush to closure.	Often delays deciding, wanting to keep things open.
May jump to conclusions and make false assumptions without checking these out with partner.	May be unwilling to commit immediately to a decision, especially if pressed by partner.
	May "undecide."

[Ps may accuse Js of acting on false assumptions without checking it out with them. Ps may feel "nailed down" by Js. Js may be frustrated by the openendedness of Ps and see them as evasive and/or rebellious.]

The preferences have been described separately but are most useful when used in type combinations. The type points to the dominant, auxiliary, and inferior functions. Characteristics listed for S, N, T, and F would be particularly true where that function were dominant and least true where the function was the inferior. For example, with dominant thinking and inferior feeling, the feeling function is primitive so it is difficult to respond with words describing emotions to the question, "What are your feelings about our relationship?" Instead, the dominant thinker is likely to respond with, "I think such and such" or supply some kind of fact about the relationship. Use of the inferior is even more difficult under pressure such as during conflict. Hesitancy and vulnerability in using the inferior function are misread by the partner as "being difficult," "not caring" and so forth. A vicious cycle of conflict emerges.

The effects of dominant and inferior are compounded when one partner's dominant is the other's inferior. The INTP-INFP couple mentioned earlier had their most difficult times around the T-F differences. Each resented the way the other approached problems and what the other saw as important. The INFP always began discussions around the nuances of their relationship, her personal emotional reactions, and questions about his emotional reactions. The INTP began by wanting to analyze the issues, focusing on ideas and facts. He wanted her to be more specific in her thinking. She saw him as cold and detached. He saw her as overly subjective. Each was trying to approach a problem with their best and trying to avoid using their inferior function, where they felt most vulnerable, especially when the relationship was at stake.

Obviously non-verbal communication will be influenced by preferences too. This is probably most apparent in the E-I dimension because of the direction of client's energy outward (E) or inward (I). Body language can confirm hunches counselors have that certain communications are received positively or negatively by partners in part because of their types. Another important form of communication is couples' sexual interactions. Sexual expression is influenced by type (Provost, 1990). "For instance, SP types may be more spontaneous than SJs in their sexual behavior. An SP involved with an SJ might become frustrated if the SJ responded to playful sexual overtures with 'Not now; I've got this report to write'" (p.84). Although spontaneity is an important aspect of sexuality, this same SJ partner may be particularly good at planning a romantic evening together and thinking of sensory specifics to enhance the experience. Sensing types are usually more naturally tuned in to their bodies than intuitive types, especially where N is dominant and S is the inferior. Therefore, sensing types' sensuality may originate with the physical, and intuitive types' with the imagination. Of course, other variables such as gender influence sexual response just as they do other aspects of communications. If counselors are working with couples about their sexual communications, it will be helpful to explore with them how their MBTI preferences affect the way they talk about sex (if they do) and how they express themselves sexually. Together they can go beyond the few examples given here to discover new ways of responding to each other.

UNDERSTANDING "FIGHT" STYLES

Below are some typical type patterns related to "fight" or conflict management styles along with suggestions for interventions. This is not an exhaustive list.

Extraversion-Introversion

Extraverts usually prefer dealing with conflict immediately and tend to be more confrontational than introverts. Extraverts are anxious to talk out the difficulty with the partner. Introverts, in contrast, generally prefer to withdraw from the conflict so they have time and space to reflect on and understand the conflict. If partners are opposite on this scale, the difficulties become obvious. The extraverted partner wants to talk about the problem *now*. The introverted partner feels "cornered" and tries to withdraw from the situation. The extravert interprets the partner's response as avoidance or unwillingness to work on the relationship. The extravert presses for immediate discussion or resolution. The introvert feeling cornered responds with either emotional counterattack or more likely with retreat and/or emotional shut-down. The Introvert sees the Extravert as controlling and demanding.

In this situation it's helpful for the counselor to do several things:

∝ Remind the partners they both share the same goal of resolving the conflict.
∝ Clarify the differing needs of E and I in the situation.

Introverts need some time and space to process the conflict internally. Introverts' best or dominant is within. To apply their best to the problem they must have reflective time. Extraverts need to realize that they will not get the best from their introverted partners by demanding immediate response. If they really push, they may get some response, but it may later be recanted or undermined because it was premature and forced. So both partners lose this way. Extraverts need assurances from their introverted partners that they will get back to them and discuss the conflict. It helps if introverts can be clear and explicit, such as "I need an hour or two to think about this, but I know you're anxious to get this settled, and I promise I'll be willing to talk about this before bedtime." Extraverts need to learn to wait for a response. Introverts need to learn to explicitly *ask* for the time they need and to state *when* they will be ready to talk. Counselors can use role-playing, homework, and other techniques to coach couples in how to negotiate conflicts.

Sensing-Intuition

Sensing partners want to fight about specifics and may even exaggerate this to "nitpicking" under stress. Intuitive partners want to argue about the *pattern* in the conflict. Intuitives may read too much into a particular conflict and see the conflict as a statement or metaphor of the *whole* relationship. While they are taking this perspective, the sensing partners are challenging them with, "What do you mean? Yesterday I did such and such." Sensing partners fight the generalities with specifics. Intuitives may dismiss the specifics as "irrelevant." A power struggle ensues about which kind of perception—sensing or intuition—is "right." Intuitive partners may project a specific conflict into a negative vision of the future with their partner, while sensing types may insist on only sticking with the here and now issue and/or referring to past history.

Again, the counselor can help partners understand the effects of the preferences in the conflict. Counselors can stress that both kinds of perception are needed to resolve problems. Using an acknowledged problem solving model (described on p.30 of *Introduction to Type* by Myers), the counselor can stress starting with sensing. Both partners together can explore, "What are the specifics?" Then they can shift to intuition and ask, "Is it possible that there is a pattern here in the specifics? Is there another way or ways to interpret this situation?" Each partner's way of seeing things is affirmed. The counselor may need to model this process and coach the couple.

Thinking-Feeling

Thinking partners can be painfully blunt in their efforts to arrive at the "truth." They may debate and argue as a means of contact with the partner. Feeling partners put a high value on harmony and may go out of their way to avoid conflict. Feeling partners are more likely to be accommodators in their relationships. Both partners pay a price for excessive accommodation. Partners with preferences for introversion and feeling tend to be the most conflict-avoidant. Partners with preferences for extraversion and thinking tend to be more confrontive.

Feeling types need to be helped to see the longer term negative effects of too much accommodation. If they fear conflict, they can be shown positive and assertive strategies for handling disagreements. They are more likely to face a conflict if they can see that some short term discomfort is less costly than long term deterioration of the relationship from avoiding conflict. Counselors can help thinking partners become more understanding of their feeling partners' responses. Sometimes a "scientific" explanation of emotions as biological facts with physiological reality is helpful.

In the previous section about communications and T-F differences, several observations were made about sources of conflict. To break a T-F stalemate both parties must acknowledge the validity of the other's approach as his or her natural preference. Each must find ways of bridging this difference.

Feeling types need to:

∝ Be less demanding that the partner use feeling language.
∝ Learn to listen closely for covert or implied emotions embedded in the thinker's language.
∝ Check out hunches about the thinker's emotional responses by saying something like, "If I were thinking such and such and said what you said, I would probably be feeling really vulnerable. Is that anything like what you are experiencing?"
∝ Try to discharge some of the expressive content of the conflict through writing or talking with a trusted friend who is a good listener before confronting the partner.
∝ Try to think about putting reactions into a cause-and-effect explanation for the partner.

Thinking types need to:

∝ Be patient with and respect the need for feeling partners to be expressive.
∝ Know that initially just listening intently is sufficient; it is not helpful to rush into problem solving.
∝ Make sure to state some appreciation for the partner besides pointing out their flaws or the "hard truth."
∝ Practice in low stress situations naming and talking about an emotion or reaction; develop an emotional vocabulary.

Counselors can guide couples to learn and practice these strategies. It's helpful to introduce some humor into this process. If the couple can laugh together about their differences, the battle is half won!

Judging-Perceiving

As described in the communication section, judging partners may press for quick resolution of a conflict, especially if also extraverted. Perceiving partners may balk or rebel or resent pressure for closure. Ps may feel they haven't got enough information or haven't thought enough about options to resolve anything. As this control issue emerges, the J partner may exaggerate J behaviors while the P partner reciprocally exaggerates P behaviors. The result is becoming locked in a power struggle; this theme may replay over and over with varying content. Judging partners may need a planned time to discuss the conflict, so P partners are wise to give them some advance warning.

Perceiving partners can:

∝ Acknowledge their partner's need for closure by giving the partner some idea about when they will be ready to work on the conflict or decide.
∝ Explain out loud to the judging partner the process the P must go through to be ready to decide, giving the J periodic updates. ("This is where I am now.")
∝ Try not to react rebelliously to a J partner's demand for closure. This reaction can evoke a parent (J)—child (P) transaction instead of the desired adult to adult transaction.

Judging partners can:

∝ Express a need for closure in such a way that it does not sound parental and hook the partner's child.
∝ Allow the P partner some room to consider options but ask for some kind of "deadline."
∝ If both partners can agree on the goal, such as satisfactory resolution of the conflict, the J partner needs to trust the P partner to keep to the goal, although the P's way will look different.

IDENTIFYING NEEDS WITHIN THE RELATIONSHIP AND LIFESTYLE

Some of the needs counselors may explore with couples are: degree of privacy, degree of intimacy or contact, degree of autonomy, sexual expression, money/materialism. Type understanding can enhance communications about these topics.

Type theory would predict that types would vary in their needs within a relationship. Some examples of general tendencies are:

∝ SJ types may need more security and predictability.
∝ NP types may need more autonomy and freedom.
∝ Dominant feeling types may need more intimacy contact and explicit expressions of affection.
∝ NF types may place a higher value on "spiritual connection" with partners.

∝ ST types may value actions taken and material evidence of caring more than verbal expressions.

Lifestyle needs surrounding work, leisure, household maintenance, couple time, and separate time are colored by MBTI preferences.

Lifestyle satisfaction is complex because of the many variables involved in addition to personality and because of the tensions between an individual's needs and the relationship's needs.

Leisure or play is an important channel for type expression and development. Leisure is also a place to balance or compensate for needs not met in work. Each partner may have different needs in this regard. Leisure also is a rich source for continued positive relationship development. Shared leisure is like "money in the bank" to be drawn upon during times of conflict. For an extensive discussion of these concepts see *Work, Play, and Type* (Provost, 1990).

IDENTIFYING POTENTIAL SOURCES OF DIFFICULTY

During premarital counseling many counselors and clergy include discussion of potential sources of difficulty because of type differences or similarities. The MBTI, however, cannot be used as a predictor of success or failure in a marriage; many other variables influence the quality of the relationship. Previous discussion in this chapter suggests areas of potential difficulty. The fewer preferences couples have in common, the harder they will have to work to bridge their differences. This does not mean, however, that the couple will not be satisfied in the relationship. Many couples report that these differences keep them on their toes and provide endless variety, fascination, and challenge. Sometimes differences in type are balanced by similarities in socioeconomic background, values, or other factors.

Counselors should not assume, however, that couples with the same or very similar types will have it easier. Although initially communication may be easier, there are potential difficulties. The couple may take each other for granted, not find enough contrast to remain stimulated, and become bored. The couple may also have the same blind spots. For example, an INFJ and INFP complained that nothing exciting happened in their lives and that their lifestyle was "too quiet" even for two introverts. Because both valued harmony and avoided any conflict, blandness characterized the relationship. Another couple, both ENFPs, found their relationship suffered because there was nothing leftover from their professional lives to give each other. Both were so pulled professionally in the outer world of possibilities that they took on too much to leave time for the relationship. They also never got around to planning vacations or specific times together. A lot of tension and avoidance surrounded necessary tasks such as household maintenance. One deceptive aspect of type that makes it important for counselors to understand type dynamics is a situation where partners have three letters in common but their functions are used in the opposite attitudes; for example, INFP and INFJ. The INFP extraverts intuition (the auxiliary) and introverts feeling (the dominant). This is reversed in the INFJ. So even though there is a sense of similarity, in actual day-to-day functioning their styles feel different. Metaphorically the couple are dancing to the same tune but starting on different feet, or experience each other as slightly off rhythm. Because the INFP's dominant feeling judgments are held deeply within, the INFJ may be surprised or bewildered at what seems like a sudden intense, absolute decision by the INFP. Both use feeling judgment but the INFJ does not put the same degree of emphasis on feeling because it's the auxiliary. Also the INFJ uses feeling to order the *outer* world as harmoniously as possible. The INFJ engages in complex internal speculation about ideas and possibilities (dominant intuition) which are then filtered in bits to the outer world through the feeling auxiliary. The INFP throws out possibilities (intuition) more freely to the partner and may struggle to grasp the entire private picture the INFJ partner holds. These differences in use of intuitive perception, for example, might make building a house together more complicated than expected.

In formulating hunches about potential difficulties, counselors can start by considering whether partners are similar or different on each of the preferences. If similar, does it result in a blind spot? If different, is there miscommunication or conflict? Then the four letter type of each should be considered to include the dynamics: which functions are dominant, auxiliary, etc. and how are these functions used (extraverted or introverted). For instance, one could expect that at some point in a long term relationship an ENTP and ISFJ may struggle about issues of autonomy and spontaneity versus security and tradition. This theme would color the way this couple evolves their style of intimacy.

APPROPRIATE AND INAPPROPRIATE USE

Cautions

The MBTI cannot save a marriage. Many other factors go into what makes a relationship work. One cannot rely primarily on the MBTI as *the* strategy of couples counseling anymore than counselors can rely solely on the MBTI with individual counseling.

Although many uses of the MBTI with couples have been described, there are occasions when its use could be detrimental. Timing and good judgment by the counselor are essential. Some reasons to hold off introducing the MBTI to a couple are:

∝ There is a great deal of blaming going on. There is the danger that one or both partners will grab their MBTI results and use them as labels to blame the other, despite careful interpretation and cautions by the counselor.
∝ There is a very unequal distribution of power within the relationship. The powerless partner feels too vulnerable to answer a personality indicator (and might not be honest if very defended).
∝ It seems likely the couple will not listen closely to MBTI explanations and will use type as an excuse: e.g. "See, I don't have to be accountable; I'm a P."
∝ There's a pressing issue in the foreground, usually a crisis, that must take precedent and be resolved before personality styles can be effectively explored.

There are some ethical issues that may arise in using the MBTI with couples. If the counselor is currently working with only one partner who has received MBTI results, that partner might ask to take the MBTI home for the other to take. The client wants to explain type to the absent partner. Counselors should always do face-to-face interpretation to verify accuracy and certainly to prevent the distortions of a biased third party's explanations. Counselors should also avoid situations where one partner feels pressured or bullied into taking the MBTI. This situation can best be avoided by the counselor discussing the benefits and concerns with a somewhat reluctant partner.

Appropriate Use

The MBTI is best introduced into couples' counseling after the counselor has assessed the couple's needs and counseling goals have been mutually established. Then the MBTI can be a helpful tool to identify points of similarity and difference in preferences, communications, decision making, and so forth. The counselor explains the purpose of taking the Indicator and asks each partner to fill it out without coaching from the other. Sometimes it's helpful to ask each to fill out a second answer sheet as they think the partner would respond. That way the counselor has both the identified type and the type perceived by the other partner. Another way which is less cumbersome is to ask each partner to guess the other's preference as the counselor explains each of the four dimensions.

Suggested steps for interpretation include:

1. Restate the reason for taking the MBTI; the importance of understanding and valuing differences.

2. Give a very brief background of the Indicator and explain the concept of "preferences" as distinct from behaviors.

3. Ask each's reactions to answering the questions; use their comments as a way to explain the dichotomous nature of the MBTI, that there are no right or wrong answers, and so forth.

4. Give each a work sheet to follow as you go through an explanation of each dimension. A useful handout is *"Verifying Your Type"* (sold by CAPT). Or use *Introduction to Type.*

5. As each dimension is explained, ask each partner to guess his/her own preference and also that of the partner. Then share how they actually came out on the Indicator. Discuss any discrepancies and watch for opportunities to tie preferences to presenting concerns. Watch for issues that should be explored in more depth, either at that moment or in future sessions. Sometimes it becomes more important to spend a whole session on one dimension or emerging issue than to push to complete an interpretation in one session. The goal is to enhance communications, not to complete the procedure of interpretation.

6. After each dimension has been discussed and the couple know their four preferences, the dynamics of the full type can be explored, including dominant, auxiliary, and inferior. They can be given *Introduction to Type* and/or books such as *Work, Play, and Type* (Provost) or *Lifetypes* (Hirsh and Kummerow, 1989) to take with them. Encourage them to read and discuss their understanding of the preferences.

7. Sometimes it's useful to give "homework" such as observing how they make a small decision together and then reporting back at the next session. Be careful to watch for couples using type as an excuse or as a blaming device. In subsequent sessions watch for misunderstandings about type concepts and look for opportunities to apply type to their issues.

EXTENDING THE PROCESS TO THE FAMILY SYSTEM

Many of the same principles can be used if the focus expands beyond the couple to the family system. Type can be of great value in helping each member of a family be better understood and to improve communications. The member who is very different in type from the rest of the family can especially be helped through affirmation of legitimate differences. When this member is an adolescent, affirming these differences is crucial in the developmental struggle to differentiate from the family and move towards psychological and instrumental independence.

Knowledge of family members' preferences can help the family better plan leisure, vacations, and daily living arrangements and make better decisions together.

COUNSELING AT VARIOUS RELATIONSHIP STAGES

Earlier we saw the value of using the MBTI in premarital counseling to educate couples to respect differences and learn communication strategies. Other couples might benefit from the MBTI later in their relationship as a form of enrichment or when the relationship becomes stuck or problematic. Couples terminating their relationship might benefit from understanding how their types may have gotten in the way of the relationship, so they can learn from their mistakes. Type understanding can help couples terminating their relationship communicate more effectively, especially important if there are children involved.

Many books have been written about the various stages relationships go through. Type and Jungian theory of the psyche's contrasexual dimension add further insight. When we say that opposites attract or that there is a certain "chemistry," often so intense as to look like addiction, we are describing what Jungians would term projection of the contrasexual aspect onto the love object/person. This contrasexual aspect is called the anima in men and the animus in women. Jung called the anima and animus "archetypes," meaning they were general forms or motifs that shaped certain personality qualities, much the way a river bed contains and shapes the flow of water. The anima/us exists in the unconscious part of ourselves and is the undeveloped, unrecognized aspects of ourselves, our unexpressed feminine or masculine side. Jung was influenced in his thinking by the Eastern concept of the yin and yang, light and dark, masculine and feminine, existing in each person. Since we cannot directly connect with the contrasexual aspect within ourselves, we develop this side of ourselves through relationship. Attraction to another is the idealization of undeveloped aspects of ourselves seen in the other. We see our love object as bigger than life and project undeveloped aspects of ourselves onto the loved one. Type differences are often part of the projection, since our least preferred functions (the tertiary and inferior) are for the most part unconscious.

Over time within the relationship we learn about the aspects that are in our own unconscious. We see these aspects modeled. We feel more complete in this relationship, because we are embracing indirectly aspects of ourselves. But the "honeymoon" stage of the relationship cannot last, because the extreme idealization of the loved one cannot be maintained through day-to-day living. The differences that attracted each become sources of conflict. This leads to a stage of disillusionment that can begin within months or years. With disillusionment come anger and resentment; anger that the loved one "misrepresented" him/herself and resentment that the loved one is merely human with flaws. A great deal of conflict is natural at this stage and may cause a couple to seek counseling.

Counselors can use type and this Jungian concept of contrasexual projection to help couples work through this stage. It seems that many couples counselors today reflect society when they readily agree that the couple's conflict represents a need to terminate the relationship. In our disposable, consumer society, we are more likely to discard relationships in the disillusionment stage than to work through the issues. Working through this stage makes it more possible for individuals to achieve intimacy and authentic love beyond love which is actually possession and control. The working through helps each partner learn new lessons about him/herself. Type affirms differences in the partner; these differences are not deliberate attempts to "hold out" or "punish" the partner. Jungians suggest that growth occurs when each partner "peels off the projections from the partner" and claims them for her/his own. In the example of a lesbian couple, if the ISTJ partner "peels off" the qualities of fun-loving spontaneity from her ESFP partner, she would claim some of that fun-loving quality as a part of herself. She would realize that she herself is capable of expressing these qualities at times, since she has come to understand and know these qualities through relationship. She, with the partner's support, can practice this expression. The result will not look like the partner's style and may not be as effective, but nevertheless is a further step in the individuation process. Her ESFP partner may "peel off" the expectations that her partner must be the one to organize and keep track of everything. Now the ESFP begins to realize her own capabilities to organize, learned in the relationship through modeling. She can claim some of this quality for herself. This process takes time, but the counselor can help set it in motion. Jungians suggest that real love between partners cannot be achieved until this stage is worked through and the partners love each other for who they really are, not for the idealized projections. To put it another way, not until the projections are peeled off and we see the partner as he/she actually is and accept that person *as is* can we begin to have true intimacy.

CHAPTER SIX

Type Patterns in Counseling: Research and Conclusions

S ome patterns are suggested by the preceding cases, but caution must be used not to make categorical statements, such as all those of a certain type present certain problems. Variations within the 16 types and other variables contribute to the complexity of human behavior. Those who seek counseling may be different in some ways from others of the same type who do not perceive a need for counseling. Many of these cases are young types, who have for the most part not had time to develop their auxiliary, third, and fourth functions. We would expect these young types to appear different in some ways from their older counterparts. In addition, these cases do not include both genders for each type, nor much diversity. Gender and diversity can modify presentation of types within counseling. In my clinical work I have found age and environment to be stronger factors than gender in variation within types.

Readiness to work with the counselor/therapist and to experiment with using MBTI functions other than the dominant are important themes in these cases. The counselor may assess the need for function development in an immature type who has little balance, but the client must agree with this counseling goal and respond to interventions in order for change to occur. Many of these clients in acute stress showed motivation to continue counseling only as long as the crisis was unresolved. Some were unwilling to try new coping skills that were not a function of their strongest preferences.

The number of counseling sessions seemed most related to the T-F preference. F clients were more likely to stay in counseling for a longer length of time, regardless of their other preferences. Type similarity between counselor and client did not seem to be a factor in the number of counseling sessions. For example, the ISFJ was more dissimilar than the ENTP to my ENFP type yet had many more sessions. Although more cases would be needed to verify a pattern in the number of sessions related to the T-F scale, two possible explanations occur to me. One is that my personality and interaction style appeal more to Fs than Ts.

Even more likely to be a factor, is that F types generally seem to have a higher need for verbalizing emotional concerns and find the counseling process more attractive than Ts do. The Ts as a whole may not trust the subjectivity they perceive to be inherent in the counseling process. Ts may be less willing to invest much time and money in counseling, which often has no quantifiable outcomes.

Certain issues and concerns seemed more common to certain types. Dependency issues seemed to be associated more with the J preference than any other. Js often need more structure and security especially in making a major transition, such as going away to college and leaving familiar support structures behind. Js do not generally shift gears or adapt as quickly as the Ps. The Ps had more difficulties in organizing themselves, developing study habits, handling procrastination, staying motivated, and learning to set priorities. Concerning the latter, Ps frequently seemed to have trouble using their judging function (T or F). The EPs among these cases tended toward unfocused, frantic, and sometimes hysterical behavior. The themes of alienation and poor social skills, whether the presenting problem or a secondary theme, seemed most present in the NTs, especially the INTs. The ENTP was the exception and behaved more like the ENFP in relation to socialization. Readers may find it interesting to compare some of these observations with their own clinical observations and to the literature on the subject. For this purpose, I've included a brief discussion of some of the findings in the literature concerning type in counseling.

TYPES IN COUNSELING

Mendelsohn and Geller (1977) reported fewer SJs and more Ns and Ps using a college counseling center. Carskadon (1979) in a research review also reported a higher frequency of Ns and NPs, especially for males; he found clinicians more frequently with preferences for N and NF. In this same research review, Carskadon notes Arain's (1968) findings of no correlation between presenting problem and type in a high school student sample. Jones and Sherman (1979) had many interesting observations about type patterns in the case load of a college counseling center. Some of these were:

∝ the most frequent type seeking career counseling was INFP;
∝ ENFPs needed academic counseling, were more rebellious and less willing to conform, and had poor study habits;
∝ students with mild or slight scores on the T-F dimension had problems making decisions.

In the counseling center I have directed, we calculated a self-selection ratio (SSR), comparing percentages of each type seen in the center compared to the percentages of the 16 types in the student body. Proportionately overrepresented in the center were: Ns (p <.01), IJs (p <.05), NPs (p <.05). Underrepresented were: Ss (p <.01), EJs (p <.05), STs (p <.01), SPs (p <.05), and ESs (p <.001). ESTJ was the least likely type to use the center (p <.01). Another SSR was used to see if certain preferences were more likely to be associated with eating disorders. We compared the proportions of each type seen for eating disorders with the proportions in the student body. A preference for Feeling was overrepresented (p <.05) in those seen for eating disorders. Gender was controlled for, since most clients with eating disorders are women.

Hawkins' (1989) study of outpatients in a mental health center found the following types overrepresented:

∝ IN and IP overrepresented (ES underrepresented)
∝ ISTJ women with major depression
∝ SF, SJ, ISFJ, ISFP women with panic disorders
∝ INTP men with panic disorders
∝ IN, INTJ, INFJ men and women with dysthymia
∝ INFJ, INTJ, INFP with borderline personality disorders
∝ INTJ, ISTJ, INFJ men with compulsive disorders
∝ EF, ENFP with histrionic symptomatology

Bisbee, Mullaly, and Osmond (1982) studying a population of psychiatric patients in hospitals and clinics, had the following observations:

∝. I, S, F or J and ISFP were more prone to depression and schizophrenia;
∝ the ISFPs were the most frequent substance abusers;

∝ manic-depressives were more frequently FJ, ESFJ, ENTP; there were few STs in this diagnostic category.

The following table summarizes types found to be overrepresented in four studies of treatment for chemical dependency:

SSR and GENDER CHEMICAL DEPENDENCY TREATMENT

	ISTJ	ISFJ	INFJ	INTJ
Luzader	m 2.2***	m, 1.8*	m 2.6**	m 2.5***
Hawkins				
Mullaly	m 1.1*,f.49*	m1.7**,f1.7**		
Emanuel	m 2.4***,f2.3***	m2.4***,f2.5***		

	ISTP	ISFP	INFP	INTP
Luzader			m3.7***,f 5.1***	m1.7*,f 5.3***
Hawkins				
Mullaly	m 1.8*, f 1.8*			
Emanuel	m1.9***	m 1.7**,f 1.8**	m 2.0**	

	ESTP	ESFP	ENFP	ENTP
Luzader				f 2.8***
Hawkins				
Mullaly				
Emanuel				

	ESTJ	ESFJ	ENFJ	ENTJ
Luzader				
Hawkins		m 2.21***		
Mullaly				
Emanuel				

[note: SSR above 1.0 indicates overrepresentation compared to expected frequencies based on Myer's high school samples, with the exception of Hawkins' study with a base of all psychiatric out-patients in his study. *=p < .05, **=p <.01, ***=p <.001] [m = male, f = female]

In summarizing all these samples, one can see that ES preferences are underrepresented. Introverted types and many IN types are over-represented as clients and in most diagnostic categories. One should use cautions in drawing conclusions about cause and effect from these data. Reported type during the time of disturbance may not be accurate for these individuals. It could even be possible that ES types have the same proportion of disturbances but do not use these kinds of treatment facilities. Since the MBTI was developed from a theory of development based on normal, non-pathological populations, it should not be used as a tool to diagnose psychopathology.

Caution should be used in generalizing from these samples which are all samples of convenience. Other variables may be affecting the findings such as the nature of treatment facility. Larger and more randomized samples must be researched before any conclusions can be drawn. Furthermore, there is still the problem of who is doing the diagnosing; perhaps the diagnostician's type may interfere with an objective diagnosis of patients/clients of different types! That is a fascinating question in itself. For example, what is "normal" for an INTP will probably be very different from the "normal" of an ESFJ.

CLIENT-COUNSELOR RELATIONSHIPS

Thompson (1977) reported a study in which similarity and difference between client and therapist were compared to perceived counseling outcomes. Counselors and clients were given the MBTI after counseling was terminated and outcome evaluations completed. Although no significant relationships were found for type when measuring clients' perceptions of positive outcomes, there was a significant relationship between type and counselors' perceptions of positive outcomes. Similarity between counselor and client on the E-I and J-P dimensions was associated with positive counseling outcomes, as perceived by the counselor.

Client-counselor differences on these dimensions were associated with decreased counselor satisfaction with outcomes.

Mendelsohn and Geller found that the more different the client and counselor, the fewer were the number of sessions. They did not find the duration of counseling to be related to type, per se. In my counseling practice, I have not found type differences between myself and clients to be the determining factor for length of therapy.

THERAPIES

Arain found that Ts preferred cognitive therapists, while Fs preferred affective therapists. In Carskadon's review, he cites several studies where Rationale Emotive Therapy decreased irrational thinking in F's but did not have the same impact on Ts. This literature suggests that

RET provided balance for Fs; this suggestion is consistent with the cases presented in Chapter Four. A sample of psychologists in the *Manual* shows the following relationships: Ts and Ss with experimental psychology, NFs with humanistic therapies, Ts with cognitive therapies.

CONCLUSIONS ABOUT TYPE AND THE COUNSELING RELATIONSHIP

It would seem that client-counselor similarity might be naturally more conducive to productive therapy and/or longer duration of counseling. Van Franz tells of Jung matching patients he referred to therapists of similar type, "with the same blind spots," because "if two idiots sit together and neither can think, they will get into such trouble that at least one of them will begin to think!" (p. 4). With type similarity there may be less of a gap to bridge in personal style and in behavior modeled by the therapist . Thus in Jesse's case, the large gap between my natural expression of playfulness (as an ENFP) and Jesse's (ISFJ) may have made it harder for her to try new behaviors. The steps may have seemed too large, like "giant steps" instead of "baby steps," and the task may have seemed insurmountable to her at times. Even when therapists are being type-conscious, it is hard to prevent their own types from coming through.

Of course, there is much to be learned from working with very different types, who frequently teach us more about our "blind spots" and weaknesses than do those who are very similar. Counselors should try to engage the client and establish rapport using the client's language, based on knowledge of client's type. I've tried to illustrate this in some of the cases. Counselors must respect differences in preference and the accompanying differences in values and attitudes. Certainly, counselors can be more effective with any type if they are aware of their own type, the inherent strengths, weaknesses, and interactive dynamics of their type with client's type.

Counselors' awareness of their own types is crucial to consciousness of personal assumptions about what constitutes "change," "growth," "good" counseling, and positive outcomes. The language of "change" and "growth" varies by type. As an ENFP, when I use those words, I'm talking about self-actualization, awareness, self-support, and responsibility. An ST might mean concrete alterations in behavior, such as losing 10 pounds. An INT might be referring to some internal shift in thinking. With some of the cases I would have set different counseling goals than the clients did. In the therapeutic relationship the counselor may challenge clients to consider other counseling goals, but clients are the ones who must decide what they want to change, and what is important in their lives. I think counselors' awareness of these issues will lead them to be eclectic, that is to have several modalities they can use effectively with different types of clients and problems. Although counselors may favor one therapeutic approach, which is probably a reflection of their own type, they should have other counseling tools. Also, counselors aware of major differences with certain of their clients might consider using a consultant similar to the client in type and/or cultural background. This consultation could offer another perspective and enhance the counseling process. Of course, if counselor and client are very similar, a consultant of a different type could also shed new light and energy on a therapeutic relationship that could get too comfortable or even stagnant. These are certainly issues for us to consider as we work with clients.

FUTURE TRENDS

MBTI users have seen a dramatic increase in professional applications of the MBTI in the past few years, but more research is needed about these applications. We hope the Indicator will be used in appropriate and ethical ways, and that clinicians will keep good data on types, interventions, and so forth. New counseling applications are emerging such as those in behavioral medicine. Weight management, stress management, and other health related programs are beginning to incorporate the MBTI. Hammer's study (1989) found type patterns in coping resources. Using the Coping Resources Inventory he found that INTPs and ISTJs had the lowest use of inventoried coping resources. ENFPs and INFJs had the highest use of coping resources. This kind of study when replicated may suggest new counseling interventions to improve physical and mental health. Other therapists are applying type to issues of substance abuse and co-dependency. Some Twelve Step programs are beginning to utilize type dynamics. Other notable increased use is in college counseling centers, in couples therapy, and in pre-marital counseling.

Very interesting developments are the Expanded Interpretive Report (EIR) and upcoming "Counselor Scoring." These variations on the MBTI incorporate Myers' research questions, not scored on Form G. The result is a series of subscales for each of the four MBTI dimensions. Therapists who do in-depth individual work will find these subscales quite useful. Some clinicians are researching the use of Form J or the Type Differentiation Indicator (TDI), which contains 296 items and additional Subscales related to development and adjustment.

We can look forward to continued debate and research about how much of our types are "hard-wired" as opposed to learned. Some researchers are making tentative connections between brain activity and physiology and preferences. Confusion continues between type and trait, causing researchers and practitioners alike to often misuse MBTI scores. Practitioners need to be clear about the differences between type and trait. Researchers must use statistical procedures, different from those used with continuous trait measurement data, to demonstrate more clearly type and the existence of dominant and auxiliary.

THE VALUE OF THE MBTI

I believe these cases illustrate the usefulness and applications of the MBTI. Of most value is the conceptual framework of the Indicator for structuring interventions and establishing a common language between client and counselor. No matter what the specific use of the MBTI, it is consistently facilitative (when used appropriately) in identifying strengths and validating the individual. The 16 types are 16 maps of developmental paths that can give counselors clues about where to look and how to proceed. I've found the MBTI particularly helpful in doing counseling outreach and prevention. Many of these cases wouldn't have come to me, or have come so soon, if that outreach had not occurred. Finally, knowledge of my own type has heightened my awareness of the whole counseling process and helped me to monitor my own behavior, assumptions and expectations.

References

Arain, A.A. (1968). Relationships among counseling clients' personalities, expectations, and problems (Doctoral dissertation, Rutgers University). *Dissertation Abstracts, 29,* 4903A-4904A. (University Microfilms, No. 68-8640)

Bisbee,C., Mullaly,R., & Osmond,H. (1982). Type and psychiatric illness. *Research in Psychological Type, 5,* 49-68.

Carskadon, T. (1979). Clinical and counseling aspects of the Myers-Briggs Type Indicator: a research review. *Research in Psychological Type, 2,* 2-31.

Cohen, J. (1992). Spouse type similarity and prediction accuracy: testing a theory of mate selection. *Journal of Psychological Type, 24,* 45-53.

Emanuel, J. (1991). Presentation at Symposium on Type and Addictions, APT IX, Richmond, VA.

Gendlin, E. (1981). *Focusing.* New York: Bantam.

Hammer, A. (1989). Psychological type and coping. Paper presented at APT VIII, Boulder, CO.

Hirsh, S. & Kummerow, J. (1989). *Lifetypes.* New York: Warner Books.

Jones, J. H., & Sherman, R. (1979). Clinical uses of the Myers Briggs Type Indicator. *Research in Psychological Type, 2,* 32-45.

Jung, C.G. (1933). *Modern man in search of his soul.* New York: Harcourt, Brace, & Co.

Jung, C.G. (1957). *The undiscovered self.* New York: New American Library.

Jung, C.G. (1962). *Memories, dreams, and reflections.* New York: Pantheon Books.

Jung, C.G. (1968). *Man and his symbols.* New York: Dell.

Jung, C.G. (1971). *Psychological types* in J. Campbell (Ed.) *The Portable Jung.* (178-269) New York: Penguin Books.

Luzader, M. (1984). Chemical dependency and type. *Journal of Psychological Type, 8,* 59-61.

Mendelsohn, G. (1966). Effects of client personality and client counselor similarity on the duration of counseling: a replication and extension. *Journal of Counseling Psychology, 13*(2), 228-232.

Mendelsohn, G., & Geller, M. (1967). Similarity, missed sessions, and early termination. *Journal of Counseling Psychology, 14*(3), 210-215.

Myers, I.B. (1980). *Gifts differing.* Palo Alto: Consulting Psychologists Press.

Myers, I.B. & McCaulley, M.H. (1985). *Manual: the construction and use of the Myers-Briggs Type Indicator.* Palo Alto: Consulting Psychologists Press.

Myers, I.B. (1987). *Introduction to type* (Revised). Palo Alto: Consulting Psychologists Press.

Pedersen, P., Draguns, J., Lonner, W. & Trimble, J. (1989). *Counseling across cultures.* (Third ed.) Honolulu: University of Hawaii Press.

Provost, J. (1990). *Work, play, and type: achieving balance in your life.* Palo Alto: Consulting Psychologists Press.

Roberts, E.E. & Roberts, D.Y. (1988). Jungian psycholgical traits and coronary heart disease. *Journal of Psycholgical Type, 15,* 3-12.

Sherman, R. (1981). Typology and problems in intimate relationships. *Research in Psychological Type, 4,* 4-23.

Stein, M. (1985). Lecture to N.E. FL. Jungian Society, Feb. 8-9, Jacksonville.

Sue, D. (1981). *Counseling the culturally different.* New York: John Wiley & Sons.

Thompson, C. (1977). The secondary school counselor's ideal client. *Research in Psychological Type, 1,* summer, 30-31.

Von Franz, M. L., & Hillman, J. (1979). *Jung's typology.* Irving, Texas: Spring Publications.

Ware, R. & Rytting, M. (1993). Shifting of type preferences under stress. Paper presented at APT X in Newport Beach, CA.

Additional Type Related Materials by the Author

Strategies for Success: using type to do better in high school and college. (1992) Gainesville: CAPT.

"Tracking Freshman Difficulties in the Class of 1993." *(1991) Journal of Psychological Type,* 21.

Procrastination: Using Psychological Type Concepts to Help Students. (1989) Gainesville: CAPT.

Applications of the Myers-Briggs Type Indicator in Higher Education. (1987), (Ed. with Anchors, S.). Palo Alto: Consulting Psychologists Press.

"Teaching excellence and type." (1987) *Journal of Psychological Type,* 13.

"Type watching and college attrition." (1985) *Journal of Psychological Type,* 9.

Note: for "Ethical Guidelines," conference and membership information: Association for Psychological Type (APT), 9140 Ward Parkway, Kansas City, MO 64114, 816/444-3500.